A Memoir In 65 Postcards
&
The Recovery Diaries

A Memoir
In 65 Postcards
&
The Recovery
Diaries

ELEANOR ANSTRUTHER

T

Troubador Publishing Ltd
Unit E2 Airfield Business Park,
Harrison Road, Market Harborough,
Leicestershire. LE16 7UL
Tel: 0116 2792299
Email: books@troubador.co.uk
Web: www.troubador.co.uk

ISBN 978 1805144 335

British Library Cataloguing in Publication Data.
A catalogue record for this book is available from the British Library.

Printed and bound by CPI Group (UK) Ltd, Croydon, CR0 4YY
Typeset in 11pt Minion Pro by Troubador Publishing Ltd, Leicester, UK

For my children

INTRODUCTION

At the beginning of 2023, having had two novels turned down, and feeling utterly morose, I decided to take matters into my own hands and join the community of writers on Substack for whom *publish* was the press of a button. At least there, in that corner of the universe, no one could say no, or stand in my way; there were, and are, no gatekeepers. After much shaking and flaking around, I settled on a practice of daily posts that would take one minute to read. I would write them first thing in the morning, I wouldn't plan, and I would publish whatever I produced. My creative energies given free flow, these daily posts became memoir pieces which coalesced into the project, *65 Postcards*. You can find the full artwork for each postcard on my Substack page: eleanoranstruther.substack.com

The memoir project finished by early summer, I took a short break, but realised pretty quickly that I was far from done, and so *The Recovery Diaries* were born. These followed the same pattern of rules: up early, no planning, make it short and snappy, see what comes out. They are a deeper investigation into the world that the memoir conjures, they are about recovery, what I can, and cannot say, a fairy story of somatic detail. They are intimate and they are universal. They are you and me.

Happily, over that year of writing, I was joined by the most important part of this merry-go-round that is, readers, you. Here's what some of you have already said…

"Too good." Sam Bain (*Peep Show, Four Lions, Fresh Meat, Babylon, The Stand In, The Retreat, Corporate Animals*)

"Anstruther gets herself all over the page. Messy, fevered and most of all compelling, her diaries are a kaleidoscope of memory, grief and hope. You can also pick up some very cool British slang if you're just a lowly yank like me." Tommy Swerdlow (*Cool Runnings, The Grinch, Puss in Boots: The Last Wish*)

"Eleanor Anstruther approaches the mysteries of life head on in a language that is both honest and breathtaking. Her writing contains darkness and light, like all the best things." Deirdre Lewis (*Snaps*)

"Thank you for sharing with us, such an exploration of yourself and all our frailty and resilience, in such luminous, perceptive prose always." A. Jay Adler (*Homo Vitruvius, Waiting For Word*)

"Eleanor's intimate and defiant essays shimmer beyond anyone else's writing… and I really do mean anyone else. She gets to the truth. The point of it all. It's gold dust." Tor Udall (*A Thousand Paper Birds*)

"A marvel of the vulnerable, the bare truth with the heartbreak of childhood and the discovery of self." Mary Tabor (*Mary Tabor "Only connect", The Woman Who Never Cooked, Who By Fire*)

"Eleanor's work reaches places that few writers reach, leaving a beautiful thread of words for her readers to follow her into the shadows and then out again into the light." Jeffrey Streeter (*English Republic of Letters*)

"An eye, and ache, and a pinch of sorcery. This prose is stunning." Adam Nathan (*Adam Nathan, Scheherazade, Actor, Finisterre*)

"My daily dose of The Recovery Diaries became more important than Wordle." Rod O'Grady (*Bigfoot Mountain, Bigfoot Island*)

"Every one of her Recovery Diaries posts feels like a Buddhist koan, a short but sweet guide to deeper understanding. I'm also calling it a memoir-in-flash, brief episodes that build up, layer by layer – a life, a heart, a woman of courage, wit, and intelligence." Troy Ford (*Ford Knows, Lamb*)

"Calling Eleanor Anstruther an Unfixed resource feels too tidy and finite. Her essays are food, prayer, solid earth and good dirt under my fingernails." Kimberly Warner (*Unfixed*)

"Over the months when Eleanor Anstruther's daily shots – her thousand-word snatches of memoir – landed in my inbox every weekday morning on Substack, I quickly became an addict. Her fearless exhumation of her past (and thus perhaps of all our pasts), and her searing, concise recreation of its traumas has stayed with me. I'm delighted to see these pieces collated in book form." Ysenda Maxton Graham (*The Real Mrs Miniver, Terms & Conditions, British Summer Time, Jobs For The Girls*)

"Eleanor writes into memory and emotion with the deftness of a conjurer. You don't read her work so much as fall into it." Julie Gabrielli (*Building Hope*)

"When I read entry #34 in The Recovery Diaries, it really hit me how powerful Eleanor's daily writing practice is. As she puts it, "the point is immediacy." There are so many words that I want to come and they change from day to day, minute to minute. It's only by having a regular writing practice that you capture all of the gems. Eleanor strings these gems together to create a necklace of insights that sparkles and shines. Whether you finger one gem or read the entire thing like a rosary, this necklace soothes and inspires." Kathryn Vercillo (*Create Me Free*)

"Awesome." Michael Mohr (*Michael Mohr's Sincere American Writing, Two Year's in New York, The Grim Room*)

"To read Eleanor's journey of recovery is to follow a brave soul with a bright lantern that illuminates even the darkest of places she's travelled. Her writing is not just luminous, but precise and direct in its rendering of memories both bitter and sweet." Ben Wakeman (*Catch & Release*)

"Upsetting in the way we all want literature to upset us. With exquisite purpose." Willow Stonebeck (*Branches*)

"Gripping, eviscerating, haunting – I woke up every morning wanting to read more, to understand better, to participate. An amazing experience and I'm very grateful to have been able to share it." Kate Beales (*writer, freelance director, arts practitioner, associate NT, RSC, Royal Albert Hall, The Watermill, Bath Theatre Royal, Salisbury Playhouse, Watford Palace, Newcastle Theatre Royal, Theatre Clwyd*)

"Eleanor's writings assist us in finding peace within ourselves." Maurice Clive Bisby (*Maurice's Substack*)

"Such a vivid, visceral, and also sensitive and soulful writer. My mind is a little bit blown every time I read her." Jenn (*Gathered & Scattered*)

"A brilliant artist." Steve Neill (*Steve Neill's SNG Studio*)

"Eleanor is feral, wild, free... Reading (her) work has

made me a better writer. She's made me more honest." Jo Vraca (*Say What*)

"So raw and relatable, and yet completely unique in voice." Dr. Kathleen Waller (*The Matterhorn: truth in fiction, A Hong Kong Story, The White Night*)

"Eleanor Anstruther writes some of the most interesting sentences I read; the sentences often contain the most interesting observations – about people especially – I encounter. I'm affected by every post." Mills Baker (*Sucks to Suck*)

"Recovery is progressive just like addiction. Eleanor keeps it moving in the right direction – now and forward!" Dee Rambeau (*Of A Sober Mind*)

"Eleanor Anstruther's writing makes you see the world with a clearer vision, and lets you fall in love with life while showing how life breaks your heart. There are passages and sentences that'll resonate so deeply, they'll take your breath away." Russell C. Smith (*The New Now*)

"I totally loved receiving her writing into my life each morning… it expanded my heart and inspired me… She speaks of the everyday and the eternal so profoundly and enjoyably, I couldn't help but read it." Sophie Knock

"65 Postcards was my absolute favourite thing to read over the summer, with its roller coaster reveals and heart-breaking insights, and I wondered at times whether the author would actually survive. Eleanor followed this with the equally affecting Recovery Diaries, tales of joy and triumph alongside sadness and fear. All life is here, as they say, and then some. Wonderful." Sally Harrop (*Sally's Substack*)

"Sometimes when you've got your head down and you're trudging along that endless path on that journey you're not sure you want to be on, you'll find some beautifully written words. Eleanor provides those words and they are like plasters for your blisters and hugs for your soul and remind you that journeys can be long but you'll get there." Lynette Clarke

"Such direct and engaging writing. I always want to know what happens next. If there were pages to turn, I'd be turning them. Putting the postcards and diaries in a book is a way to give the reader back that power." Toria (*Toria*)

"Powerful, dreamlike, and potent." B. Robin Linde (*Odd Positive*)

"This year's expression of struggle, perseverance and light at the end of the tunnel. Well worth every moment of reading." Mel Forsyth (*Crack Daddy Wanted*)

A Memoir In 65 Postcards

1

A JOURNEY TO INDIA

When I was eighteen, I met a boy who told me a story of being kidnapped from his mother when he was four years old. He was taken to England by his father, never to see her again. In my mind I saw a room in southern India, gossamer curtains, a broad messy bed of white sheets, a mother sleeping with a child in her arms. I saw a man creep in, he was a pilot so I put him in pilot's uniform, no jacket. I saw him lift the boy from his mother's arms, the curtains stirring gently in the breeze, the mother waking hours later, her horror shock of emptiness. The boy and I were in our second year at Manchester University. He'd come over to the house in Withington, I'd opened the door and about two seconds later was going out with him. I remember the night he told me; we were in bed and as his story unfolded I unfolded my limbs from around him. His parents had been on their way to Brazil from Australia when their flight touched down in Karnataka to refuel. They got out to stretch their legs, the loud jungle calling them, and came upon the abandoned house of a colonialist, pidgins making the frightening cacophony of escape as they pushed open the door, holding vines aside. The shock of a man hanging in the hall, his last breath there. This was enough to make them stay, abandon their plans; she was a nurse and one place was as good as another to set up a village hospital. They never reboarded their flight to Rio. The house of the dead colonialist became their home. That was the story he told me. I said, *We have to go.* It was too obvious. So we dropped out and bought flights to Mysuru, took buses and rickshaws, heading towards Srirangapatna, the village of his birth. We asked and asked and on the final day of searching a tuk-tuk driver said yes, he knew her. I remember feeling petulantly grumpy as we walked the last dusty mile, self-centred as the epic reunion took place – he, knocking on the door, she, opening it. I was hot and tired. It had been all about him. I went for a swim in the river and slipped on stones and got frightened by giant, scuttling crabs. I crossed the unkempt lawn and shook her hand, sat on the wide veranda, gossamer curtains lifting in the breeze. We stayed for months, bought a motorbike and converted it for the long road north. The story of that journey I wrote into my first novel. It sits in a drawer, a great title but not much else to recommend it.

2

HE TOOK THE BIKE

My boyfriend and I took off on the motorbike, a Royal Enfield Bullet heavy with luggage, and purring. We headed first to meet his brother – also estranged until now – for a few nights of giant beetles flying into my hair and then north up the Western Ghats. The monsoon chased us. We'd mistimed our travels and no matter how fast we rode, the rains caught up. We stopped soaked and freezing in tea plantations, couldn't undo the swollen ropes that tied our soaking gear to the bike, slept in roadside rooms fully clothed, never time to dry off. In Goa we looked for the parties that had already moved north. At the Taj Mahal we sat on marble away from each other. In Delhi we put on helmets and couldn't see for moths. In Rajasthan we fell in love with green-eyed women and crashed the bike in sand. In Chandigarh we slept in a barn with twenty men, one of whom put his hand down my jeans again and again until I woke my boyfriend up and told him we had to leave. He agreed, but grudgingly; we weren't friends, he and I. Already we were unhappy. From the night he unfolded the story of his kidnap to the last dusty road to his mother's house had been a matter of months. We'd left England on an impulse, no plan except to find her. And we were children; we hardly knew ourselves let alone each other. At a chai stop in the foothills of the Himalayas we met an Israeli couple who invited us to stay. They had a Royal Enfield too. It had got us talking. We followed them, two Bullets chugging up the winding narrow roads of the valley towards Manali, the great drop to our right, the apple trees bending in the light, sudden rainbows bowing to drink from the river crashing below. They parked at a cow shed above which were some rooms. We followed them up the wooden steps. He cooked a meal on a camping stove, tomatoes, onions and green peppers. She unfolded their clothes and made the bed. We ate and then they gave us acid and suggested an orgy. I remember thinking, *How revolting.* My boyfriend also declined. We went to bed listening to them laughing. The next day a friend of theirs arrived, the most beautiful man I'd ever seen; tendrils of dark hair, a soft pink shirt, faded jeans, he sat cross-legged on the floor and passed me a chillum. My boyfriend went out to get food. When he came back, he found us together. I gave him only the most fleeting of goodbyes. He took the bike.

3

MUTE

The Israeli was handsome and unkind. I grew fat on German pastries, he poked my backside and said so. His cool Israeli friends came over and sat about smoking chillums; a complicated series of rituals which I got wrong. How to mix the charas and tobacco in your palm, how to pack it and wrap your special ragged cloth about the base, the *boom shanker* throw of a prayer and touch to the forehead, how to light it, get it burning without dying, breath in without throwing a whitey, and for god's sake don't pass it to the left. I pretended to know everything while wishing I spoke Hebrew. I think I thought I was happy. I'd cut ties from England, taken off on my own, taken up with a man who'd done military service, who'd stripped out of his uniform and grown his beautiful hair; I felt grown up. We took LSD and walked amongst the apple trees. He taught me how to cook shakshuka. When he went out, I sat in the window and wrote my diary, smoked spliffs and listened to Edie Brickell. The cows beneath our rooms rang their bells at night. We spent three months in the mountains of Manali and then the seasons changed and we took the bus to Goa. He rented a house in Arambol. A mosquito net over our bed caught scorpions which he killed with a stick. Pigs chased us through bamboo for a feed on our morning faeces. Water was pumped from the village well and carried in buckets, and his friends, more of them, gathered on our porch. Circles of handsome women and confident men, they moved effortlessly, sat carelessly, knew the rules; not tourists but travellers, they made that distinction in every sweeping statement about Indian life. I swept the floor and made the bed and fetched water from the well. We went to a full moon party on the beach. My handsome and unkind Israeli gave me a microdot. His friends played djembe and threw back their heads at the stars. I ran down to the water's edge. Thousands of stone soldiers were marching from the sea. I said, *Look!* and he said, *Why do you think I see what you see? You are on your own* and he left me there. A night tripping without anchor, I set sail and didn't come back. The sun rose, we returned to our house and life together. Like a mute maiden he'd picked up at the market, my body continued to sweep the floor and fetch water, cater to his beautiful friends on our porch but my mind was gone. I stopped speaking.

4

LOST GIRLS LIKE ME

I found my voice in the hands of a self-styled Colonel Kurtz on an island in the Gulf of Thailand. A White man running from something, he'd decided himself a temple father, fat under a palm tree handing out easy wisdoms to lost girls like me. My Israeli and I had gone to Bangkok to renew our Indian visas; with our passports stamped we travelled out to the islands for a bit more beach life, Colonel Kurtz was a friend of his. I remember almost nothing of the time we spent there except for sitting at the feet of that large, sweating man. My months of mute had made me invisible yet suddenly I felt seen. He told me I was special. That old chestnut. Classic. By the time we left I was speaking again and my Israeli had found God. We returned to our house in Goa where full moon parties were replaced by Friday night prayers. A cloth on my head, he no longer taught me how to load a chillum but how to move my hands in circles over candles, repeating Hebrew texts he knew by heart. His friends came over, but less often. The drugs stopped. I swept and cleaned and cooked and lay beneath him. I broke my collarbone carrying water from the well and accepted this new reality as I'd accepted every other; no longer a teenager on a motorbike or the girlfriend of tendril hair, now I was a good Jewish wife who wasn't Jewish or his wife but I was adjustable, loyal, hoodwinked; I'd do anything for attention. It never occurred to me to leave. When the seasons changed, we travelled to Delhi and lay hot in our hotel bed, his arm around me. The mattress was thin, the city loud, he told me he was leaving. He was giving up this life of faded pink shirts, he was returning to Israel and his faith. I couldn't believe it was over. The next morning we parted; I flew to London, to my mother's house, he to Tel Aviv, to his. I walked barefoot through streets of my childhood, a lungi wrapped like a turban round my head. I spoke pidgin English to street people who looked at me like I was weird. I don't know what my mother thought. All I could think about was him. Across the park were synagogues still and quiet in Regency rooms. I made an appointment. I found myself there. I said I wanted to convert to Judaism. A Rabbi sat me down.

5

A MOMENTARY FLICK
OF THE SWITCH

I sat with the Rabbi in his plush, Regency room, red cushions, a view of the park. I told him I wanted to convert to Judaism. At school I had sided with the Jewish girls, opted for Jewish prayers instead of Christian, I felt that those beginnings at a private girls' school on Harley Street had come full circle, it was meant to be. I told the Rabbi I was committed. My feet were bare, he was kind, he said love wasn't enough of a reason. He sent me away to long for my Israeli in the stark uncomfortable spare bedroom of my mother's tall, uncomfortable house. I sat at the desk facing the window and made necklaces from beads brought home from an Indian market. I didn't talk to my family and they didn't talk to me. Days passed. Weeks of silence. I was unthinkably absent from my surroundings. I was terribly sad. One day, unable to contain the loss, I picked up the phone and rang him. I remember the telephone in its alcove, the carpet beneath my feet, the sudden and unexpected jolt of his voice. I told him I missed him and incredibly I heard him say he missed me too. This was enough, the only invitation I needed, it was like pressing go on a racer who has leant against the starting rope, ears trained for the pistol. I was off. That afternoon I went to a travel agent near the station and bought a plane ticket to Israel. I came home and packed a bag. I imagined a life of headscarves and simplicity and picked up my sewing machine, too. Money allows for these things; a momentary flick of the switch, a plane ticket bought, no conversations had with anyone but him. I told no one. I took a taxi to the airport, a folded note on the kitchen table for my mother that I thought she'd find at breakfast. It said, *Gone to live in Tel Aviv.*

6

OH HOW THEY LAUGHED

I rang him from a payphone in the arrivals hall. I hadn't told him I was coming. I saw him weaving through the crowds of families reunited, suitcases, children, the sunshine of Israel glinting through the glass walls. He wore a yellow T-shirt. Sensible trousers. His tendrils of black hair were gone. For the first time I noticed his eyes were a little too close together. He took me by the arm and took me to his mother's house where I sat at the table not able to understand the rapid conversation, his mother shelling beans and smiling occasionally but not in welcome, there was pity there already. He got me a hotel room. He explained, as he sat on the bed, that when he'd said he missed me he hadn't meant *missed me* as if he wanted me to come. He said there was no way I could stay. He had devoted himself to his Orthodox faith, no amount of love or conversion would ever make me worthy, and he didn't love me anyway. I was wrong on every count but especially the counting up of feelings on his fingers as he took off his trousers and pushed my head down. My sewing machine sat in the corner. My bag I'd packed forever.

I slept alone in a single bed and in the morning returned to the airport. At customs the military questioned this twenty-four-hour stay in their country; I had a stamp for Morocco in my passport from a trip long ago, they didn't believe my explanation of why I'd been there or why I was leaving Israel so soon after arriving. They asked if I was a spy. I had to call my Israeli who wasn't mine anymore, who never had been. I telephoned him from the payphone again, this time to come down to the airport and tell them a story of a stupid girl who'd bought a flight on a whim, who'd got the story of love all wrong. The military personnel thought it was the funniest story they'd ever heard. It must have been the way he told it. Oh how they laughed as I stood there, bag at my feet, sewing machine heavy in my hand. They waved me through, I'm not sure the Israeli said goodbye. When I got home, I found the note I'd left on the kitchen table unopened. At supper that night my mother asked, *How was your day?*

7

A PARTY IN A HURRICANE
(OR HOW TO GET A BOY)

Home was a tall, cold house in London; intellectual, artistic, my father a writer, my mother an architect, guests, lodgers, friends and strangers, the bedrooms full of us and them, paintings on the walls, politics at the table. I moved amongst it all being pretty and clever, a seventies childhood of lentils and greens and feeling unseen, the house too full, my mother too busy, my father rarely there. I went to the local ILEA, The Marlborough, my mother was a governor. I was the only pupil in my year who lived in a private house. Everyone else came from the council flats across the road. I remember this because when I made the mistake of inviting a friend over, rumour spread in the playground that I lived in a museum. I hated school. I was lonely and uninspired. For a short time lovely Mrs Turner let me sit with her in the library learning to read but this was soon rumbled and I was thrown once again into the bear pit of the English state school playground, British Bulldog, Kiss Chase, and porn mags in the outside toilets. At eleven I went to Queen's College, a private girls' school, and started smoking. At thirteen I started clubbing, the Wag, The Mud, the Opera House and Heaven. I don't remember who came with me but I remember my brown dress, tight and dangerous on a dark West End street, waiting for the night bus home. From Queen's I went to Westminster, a place of six hundred boys and thirty girls. Day one in Little Dean's Yard had boys' faces at every window choosing who would be theirs; I looked up and decided which would be mine. My sister asked me to water the plants in her flat while she went to America. I told everyone I was having a party. My father was supposed to be leaving for France that night. He kept his car in the garage below. He owned the flat. There was scaffolding on the building opposite. The party started, hoards came, many more than I'd invited, teenagers from other schools, word had spread. We barricaded the door but they hung off the scaffolding and threw bottles at the window. They kicked the door in. The music raged, bodies pressed, none of this bothered me; I was sixteen and only interested in the boy and the hurricane inside. I didn't notice outside the wind that raged across England, tearing the land apart, stopping the ferry with my father on it from leaving.

8

I REMEMBER THAT HURT

His footsteps on the stairs, not the boy (I'd got him) but my father whose ferry had not left for France because of the hurricane that had ripped through England, ripping it apart. He'd turned his Porsche around and returned to London, parked it in the garage below my sister's flat and seen the door kicked open. I was on my knees when I saw his feet, his shoes, looked up, saw him. I was scrubbing carpets in the wreckage, graffiti on the kitchen walls, the cooker pulled out, the fridge on its knees, a window smashed, the bathroom door off its hinges, furniture sideways, the stench of sick and cigarettes and beer and sex and teenagers who'd run off into the night. He didn't talk to me for a long while after that. He'd say on the few occasions we'd be at the same table, *Please tell her to pass the salt*. And when it was my eighteenth birthday he stood in the hall and said, *I've come up for your sister's birthday so I won't bother coming up for yours.* But I'd got the boy, which was what I decided I cared about. A summer passed, my A levels passed, he must have forgotten it's a bad idea to give a riotous girl in need of attention the keys to anywhere because when I was free from school forever, he gave me the keys to the house in France. I invited all my friends and some who weren't my friend at all. We drank champagne in the sun and wine on mopeds and piled dirty plates in bin bags that we left out the back. We threw all the sunbeds in the pool. The idiot boys who were not my friends invented a game of shaming anyone who went to bed first by hauling barrels of water up the stairs and tipping them over the sleeping person. The beds were soaked, the mattresses ruined, the floor dripped through the ceilings below. We broke everything and left without clearing up or saying sorry. He didn't talk to me for many more years after that, and I remember that hurt. But I was off, away from home, from France in disgrace to Italy, Spain, Morocco and soon, Zimbabwe.

9

A MAGNIFICENT
AFRICAN SUN

A bunch of White, English, public-school kids off to teach in Zimbabwe. What could possibly go wrong. We gathered at Heathrow, I said goodbye to my mother, we flew to Harare via a skidding touchdown in snowy Sofia. At a farmstead we put up our brand-new tents and drank beer and tried out our thin camping mattresses on each other as if we were still in Chelsea. We met the priest in whose care we were placed. Also White, but large and old, he'd been a master at Sherborne. He read out the list of our pairings, strangers to each other, the person we'd spend the next year with, in a place we'd never been, mine was tall and angular, we'll call him Willy which was nothing like his real name but was the nickname he preferred. Separated into our pairs we were sent off to our schools, Willy and I among the last to go, our village was in the south. A flatbed truck delivered us to Dhirihori late at night when the stars were out and the pub open. Willy jumped off the back and settled on the stone steps with a beer, making friends. I shouldered my rucksack to the low block of rooms across the way, tin roof, concrete veranda, a door that didn't lock, one window. I'd packed according to the list: a paraffin stove, malaria pills, a water filter, sleeping bag, I'd added a pen that wrote upside down. I don't know what scenario I imagined where that would come in handy, but here's the important bit: my family are landowners, we have always owned the view. I slept on the floor and when I woke and opened the door, I remember thinking it was the first time in my life that the land outside my bedroom wasn't mine. That was the extent of my experience of the world outside a tall, cold house in London. I had not the faintest idea what I was walking into. Our headmaster took one look and knew what we were made of. He was small and didn't want us there, these ignorant White children come to fill in a year-off checklist at his school. He gave us what we deserved, the most glancing attention. As opposed to the White priest who liked to turn up in our village when the day was done and the magnificent African sun sent slanting rays across the grass. He would park at our hut, arrange picnic chairs on the concrete veranda and pour two glasses of champagne, one for him and one for me.

10

NOT OUT OF AFRICA

Of course I had the outfit. What fool would go to Africa without a long swishing skirt and cowboy boots? I believed I was all set. During the week I stood before thirty children and tried to teach them things I thought I knew; the alphabet, how to spell *definitely.* In my hut I learnt to make dinner with one pot, a relentless vegetable stew that Willy eschewed for beer at the pub with the friends he'd made and I hadn't. I marked workbooks with the pen that never had to write upside down. I listened to Simon & Garfunkel sing 'Homeward Bound' and the tap dance of lizards on the roof. At weekends I ran off to Harare at the expense of a friend of my fathers who owned a large hotel in the city. Photographs show us, the friends I had made, with white towels like turbans on our heads in plush rooms and beside a rooftop swimming pool drinking wine, aware but not ashamed of our privilege. Letters written home to my parents are gushingly dramatic, an awful lot of *missing you terribly* and *there's something in the air here making all emotion doubly powerful.* Over the Easter holidays I toured

Botswana with another friend and her family. Throughout the first and second term the White priest with his picnic chairs and champagne came and went. My boots leaked and I caught bilharzia. The pills didn't work and I caught malaria. Milk warmed on the paraffin stove gave me brucellosis. The long skirt which swished so pleasingly through the grass picked up tick-bite fever. And one morning while readying to walk from my hut to the low school buildings across the way a pain in my abdomen knocked me to the concrete floor. I remember someone running for the man who owned a car and being driven to the town where the White priest lived. The priest knew a surgeon, a mass of wild Scottish hair who was drunk from midday to collapse but catch him between hangover and beginning again and he could do all right under bright lights. In a hospital he removed my burst appendix. I woke in the priest's house hours later, my left arm black with ants that had found me sleeping, a scar above my right hip, a bottle of whisky on the table beside me.

11

FORGETFUL

My mum, who hates planes, who has a fear of flying, who at this very moment is lying in a hospital bed in the endgame of life, did something reckless and caring and got on a plane and landed in Harare and found me at the priest's house up to my neck in painkillers, sleeping pills and whisky. The priest, large and fat, who liked to make out his pillar-ness in the community, had a wife who was small and nice with bobbed hair but who turned a blind eye, she must have, how else could she stay with his wrongness, his plying young girls with champagne when they were upright and drugs and whisky when they couldn't get out of bed. I told my mum that he wasn't the nice guy he said he was but she didn't believe me, which was more to type than jumping on a plane, and the three of us, leaving his wife behind, went to his farmhouse in the countryside. That night he crept into my room carrying his bible and lay on top of me while my mum slept in the room next door. I remember the weight of him. I remember the heat of his breath. I was asked recently by a young woman who hasn't had experience of these things (is she one of the few?) why I didn't do anything, say anything, run. I explained this: there are four responses to a traumatic event – fight, flight, freeze and faun – and which we choose is a matter of pathology. Any one of them is an answer to the question of how, in that moment, to survive. Mine was to freeze. I did nothing, I said nothing, I waited for him to leave, which he did, shuffling out with his bible under his arm. We returned to his house in town the next day where his bob-haired wife waited, probably baking, being small, finding her own answer to that question. My mum and the priest had supper in the garden together. I watched from the kitchen, unable to join them. Then my mum and I went on a tour of Zimbabwe, getting soaked at Victoria Falls, having picnics on dry yellow grass in the shade of Acacia trees, marvelling at Baobabs, weaving along roads rutted with elephant tracks and then she delivered me back to the priest's house and flew home. She lies in a hospital bed now, forgetful of all these things and if she remembered them, would remember them differently. She is seeing snakes curl the curtain runners above her head, she is seeing rats run across the ceiling and draw pictures with their eyes.

12

A BAR THAT NEVER CLOSED

My friends got me out. Realising I was missing from the weekends in Harare they came to see me. I remember Eddy, who wanted to be a policeman one day, sat on the floor in the hall while I faced the priest in his kitchen. He heard me tell the priest that I would report him, and he heard the priest reply no one would believe me, which turned out to be right. But my friends got me out and we went to a Bhundu Boys concert in a stadium outside the city that was too small for the crush, that shut the gates leaving us on the wrong side of a riot. Four stupid White kids in a place they shouldn't have been, heading for a beating; my watch was ripped from my wrist as I clung to Eddy, huge beside me, ripping his jumper rather than risk letting go. Willy climbed on the roof of a taxi to shout for us, Eddy picked me up and carried me over the crowd. Willy and I headed back to Dhirihori where our headmaster met us at our rooms. He said he'd had enough, we were fired. We packed what we could carry and walked the twelve kilometres to the tarmac road and hitchhiked from there, I don't remember where. My boyfriend from

England (who I'd got with, in a hurricane) came out. Photographs show us travelling; we are waiting for lifts, a book in his hands, the road stretching sandy and sunny. We are damp in the back of a flatbed truck, heading for the border at Beitbridge. I am smiling on a beach in Durban. There are snapshots of a speedboat in the Okavango Delta, friends grinning from a ledge above Victoria Falls. We swam in Mana Pools unaware of the crocodiles. I went canoeing down the Zambezi, hippos snorting and spent the night with a South African guide. (I don't remember where my boyfriend was.) Years later I would return to the Zambezi, to an island in that river where a party held me captive for ten days, unable to leave for the drugs and a man who had cracked, but that was to come and at nineteen, canoeing and hitchhiking and smiling on a beach, I was at the beginning. We found our way to Malawi, to a hut on Monkey Bay, to a bar that never closed. I got a job. We smoked a lot of pot. We paraglided in rainbow-striped life jackets. I have an image of us side by side in the shade of a bamboo roof, he is reading, I am writing my diary. We are sun-kissed, beautiful, our days idyllic. I loved him.

13

BLACKOUT

Let's roll forward. It's 1990, Manchester. I am in my first year at university, not yet living in the house where I would meet the boy who'd been kidnapped by his father from his mother's arms. I am in Fallowfield halls of residence, three flights up from the smooth walkways of campus. The Haçienda is open but I haven't been there yet. I'm trying to fit in and forget about the boy who is no longer my boyfriend, who said when we got back from Zimbabwe, *I think we should split up now*. I've written a suicide note with no real intention of dying. I'm trying to imagine if throwing myself onto those smooth walkways from three flights up will end this loneliness. I've slept with other boys without asking their names for the same reason. Tonight I'm throwing a dinner party. I've planned roast lamb and gone to the butcher to buy it. But standing amongst racks of carcasses, the smell of sawdust and sinew, I feel faint. I think I'm going to throw up. I take the leg of lamb wrapped like a baby in paper. I run from the butcher's, the nausea subsides, evening comes. The dinner is on, the lamb is in the oven, I'm setting the table when shock like a burst appendix but worse slices through my belly. My flatmates put me on my bed. I try and climb out of the window for real this time, now to stop a pain that obliterates the pain of loneliness like the smooth walkways obliterate the grass. My flatmates hold me down and call for an ambulance. I remember the lights flashing three flights below, I remember the siren. At the hospital, student doctors are invited in to witness what is happening to me. They crowd at the end of my bed, a line of white coats and clipboards, their faces young and frightened. They are there when my fallopian tube gives up its efforts to keep itself together, sending the embryo that has been quietly growing there free falling. In Malawi I'd gone out on a boat with a man who turned out to have no intention of fishing. I'd jumped ship and walked back to my hut to find my possessions gone, everything except my passport but including my washbag which had inside it my contraceptive pills. I'd thought, *To hell with it* and carried on sleeping with my boyfriend. Now in a hospital bed in Manchester, machines beeping, roast lamb burning, student doctors taking notes, that fallopian tube is exploding. Blood fills my eyes like a cartoon. Blackout.

14

FLESH AT THE HAÇIENDA

Who knew that a bursting fallopian tube would burst the sense of what's the point? I woke up with the gloves off, a nineteen-year-old in a raver's paradise, Manchester at the height of her powers. The hospital ward of pink fluffy slippers and women with no wombs held me for a week of painful recovery. My mother came to see me. So did the boy. And then I put on my brown corduroy hotpants and Minnie Mouse platforms and went out to Flesh at the Haçienda. I think this was the first time my heart touched rave. I think I knew, immediately, I had found my love. I found a puppy on the way home too; it was crying in the gutter. We picked it up, named it Flesh and gave it to my godfather who renamed it Flash for the preference of shouting it in West London. I took revenge on the boy who'd made me pregnant, who'd been my love and left me for the buffet of university girls, by having an affair with his brother. I broke his heart. Sorry about that. I've always felt bad about it. Meanwhile the drugs of the early nineties exploded like my tube; the first time I took ecstasy at Naked Under Leather I raised my hands to the crystal teardrops cascading from the ceiling. A large Liverpudlian boyfriend gave me my first acid and was sweet and gentle in my enthusiasm to recite Yeats on a swing in the park. I got into playing squash on speed. I did no work. In my second year I moved into a house in Withington where my friends wrote essays while I ate instant macaroni from the corner shop. They went to lectures, I watched *Neighbours*. It was fun and absent and what's the point so when the boy arrived with the story of being kidnapped, I was ready. Who needed university, a degree, even another night at the Haçienda when there was *this* adventure waiting to be had? No other excuse was needed. We packed our bags and bought our flights. I'm not convinced I told my mother. When I went to my tutor to tell him I was dropping out he had no idea who I was.

15

TOO FUCKING SERENE

A photograph was sent to me last week by a Dakini goddess. She didn't know I was writing this memoir, could not have known that the photo would arrive precisely at the point where the story and image coincide. Isn't that beautiful? This process brushes with magic. Such is the way of digging and time travel. On the day it was taken I'm drifting arm in arm with my friend through the Harvest Fair, it's Lamas 1994, already I divide the year into pagan eighths. I'm returned from India and losing my mind. I'm back from twenty-four hours in Tel Aviv. The note that my mother never opened is thrown away. For a while I'd sat at the table in the window of the green spare room in my mother's tall, cold house and strung Indian beads into necklaces. One day I took them to a craft fair at Chelsea Town Hall. There I met a girl who gave me the address of her boyfriend who opened the door in a towel and invited me in, did tarot, said he was moving into a new place and I should come with. Which I did, leaving my mother's green spare room for a small, warm house in West London. A stray, I didn't ask if I could have a room, I just made camp in a hall off the kitchen and hoped they wouldn't notice or mind; these strangers who became friends, became family. I bought a pink split-screen camper that I saw parked on the street. My note left on the windscreen, *Please can I buy this van?* coincided with one the owner had left on a Porsche the same day and so he said, *Yes.* My friend and I set off together on a summer of festivals, fly-pitching our jewellery on the blankets we wore round our shoulders. As we wafted through the Harvest Fair arm in arm a woman shouted, "Too fucking serene," and we laughed and that's how we felt; on a cloud of things working our way, life slotting into place, the sun always shining. That night we took mushrooms, two hundred of us in a yurt on Lamas and the music played and the people sang and I leaned against a man who, in four years' time, I would marry in a pagan wedding. But I hadn't met him yet, only leaned against him as the yurt took off and two hundred people span in a mushroom universe. When the summer ended my friend and I parted, she to Mexico and I to Glastonbury where a man in a pottery with blonde pigtails waited.

16

THIS KING OF GLASTONBURY

It seems these are a litany of relationships gone wrong, choices made to do with men and not to do with me. That's what happens when you write a memoir. A thirty-thousand-foot view, you get to see the pattern of the streets. That summer of 1994 I was supposed to be starting an artist's collective with the girl I'd met at the Chelsea Town Hall. We'd had it all mapped out. There was a building off Portobello that we were about to sign the lease on, we'd had meetings with financial advisors, we were going to be the answer to artistic poverty. Then the man with pigtails happened. Glastonbury was a detour, a final stop on a beautiful summer before returning to London to get on with it, but no one had told me about the Tor. As I drove towards town it came up on my right, this outrageous Somerset monument, a marker on the land. I veered right up the narrow street past the Chalice Well, parked at the bottom of the hill amongst the other camper vans. At the top of the Tor I met a girl who said she had a friend in town, we should go, he'd give us tea. She led me to the courtyard on the high street, up the steps to a pottery; he was tall, thin, angular, his hands patterned with dust, blond hair to his waist plaited into two long pigtails. Leftfield boomed from the CD player. He smiled and offered me a lump of clay. In those days I didn't know the difference between connection and boundaries. I thought if the feeling was there, I must make myself available, this was destiny calling, who was I to get in the way. We made chai pots; he invited me to dinner. I followed him to his farmhouse on the Somerset Levels; a ragged kitchen, low doorways, a fireplace you could sit in, a yellow Labrador. We stayed up for three nights talking. I rang my friend in London, told her the artist's collective was off. She was furious and took twenty-five years to forgive me. I made one trip in my camper van to collect all my stuff from the happy house in West London. I moved in with this man who I didn't know but thought I did, into his life, his farmhouse in Avalon, this king of Glastonbury who had a finger in every pie. I thought, *This is it*.

17

SHE CAME TO STAY

I'd been searching for something and as far as I knew, in this farmhouse on the Somerset Levels, I'd found it. Security, safety, a home of my own with me and him; in my mind I was in bliss. For six months I cooked and cleaned and fed the dog, made candles for the candle shop, labelled bottles for the incense shop, fired chai pots in the pottery, struck up friendships in the high street, fetched water from the Chalice Well. I watched his mind at work and thought it brilliant, watched his hands describe the mathematics of business and thought him the king of Glastonbury. He had a daughter from an earlier marriage gone wrong, his wife was a traveller, their child lived with him on and off, she was sweet but I don't remember much mothering on my part, I was practically a child myself. We made a horoscope bed in the garden for his herbs and planted them according to the moon. We cleared brambles and had bonfires. Where his land ended and the levels began, he'd built a low stone circle. Beside it was a yurt, green and damp. Murmurations swept across the glass Isle of Avalon, my father came to tea and named him Pigtails. Supper at the scratched kitchen table, ducking our heads to see out of dusty windows, the floor uneven, books falling over on shelves and in the evenings, we'd settle in the sitting room, he in his armchair smoking and reading, and I in the nook of the enormous fireplace writing and rolling joint after joint. We flew to Goa for Christmas and danced on the beach, banishing ghosts he wasn't aware of. We came home and he told me about a girl who was coming to stay. I was yet to read my Simone de Beauvoir. She was the daughter of a friend. He'd been at her birth. He said, *You'll love her*. He said they were two peas in a pod. I remember the day she arrived. Her lean in the doorway of the kitchen, I in the sitting room saying hello. The confidence of her. The smile as she took me in. Her black hair and rosy cheeks. The immediate command. He was thirty-five, I was twenty-three and she was seventeen.

18

AN INCH OF ME

They moved me out in inches. It began with a mushroom trip. Pigtails and the girl, two peas in a pod went out under the stars arm in arm. I saw them seated on a log in the herb garden that he and I had built. I left them to it. I told myself I was being mature. They stayed up, or at least out, all night. I know this because he didn't come to bed. And the next morning when I saw them in the kitchen, leaves in their hair, ruffled as if they'd slept on grass, there was a smile to them. I cooked and cleaned and fed the dog, pulled weeds, smoked pot. John Lennon taught me how to make lasagne; a voice channelled in my head, don't ask me what it meant. It meant lasagne. I heard his voice and followed his recipe and Pigtails and the girl said something had been discovered. They said I should move into the spare room. Like the good girl that I was, I listened to them through the wall. The girl's mother arrived and moved into the yurt at the end of the garden. She said they'd always been like this. Inseparable. I set to clearing the vegetable patch; nettle roots straining my arms, leaves stinging my hands. My back hurt. I cooked and cleaned and fed the dog and stood outside for a UFO to flash its lights upon my head and as suddenly be gone. Pigtails said his love for me was unconditional. He said, *Couldn't we all live together?* and suggested I move into the yurt. The girl's mother gave me scabies. I itched through terrible spring, slept beside that terrible mother in a damp and leaking yurt and cooked and cleaned and fed the dog and lived this ménage à trois because all I could hear was him saying, *Don't go,* and all I could see was my grip upon this life and all I could feel was my love for him, this man who deserved not an inch of me. My back hurt more. I got sciatica. One evening the girl and I were alone. She said, *You'll never win.* I hadn't realised it was a competition. I'd thought it was a problem of my heart, that it wasn't big enough, *that I couldn't love unconditionally like he could.* That absolute fucker. I'd been taking my spine to healers, asking them, why the pain, believing they could make it better. I'd thought the hurt snaking down my leg was my inability to let her in. But the tension that had me crouched at night clutching my leg to my chest was not a signal from the universe that I was small-minded, it was my vertebrae giving up, my body saying enough, my disc about to slip.

19

GASLIGHTING

"Relationship? What relationship? You were just renting a room." Gaslighting hadn't reached Somerset in 1995 but even if it had I'm not sure I'd have named it, I was that shocked. In his kitchen, the uneven floor and books falling over, the dog looking up at me, I'd made the mistake of naming that other thing, heartbreak, betrayal, cruelty. He looked at me and I looked at him and only one of us was brazening it out. I went to stay with my friend at Longleat, a yurt dry and mossy hidden from the tourists where I slept to the roar of lions. My friend was building a stone circle for Lord Bath. He'd built the one at Glastonbury festival, he'd built the one in the garden I had left. He told me, *He doesn't love you,* as firm and solid as the stones he handled. I tripped as I went from yurt to kitchen fire and almost fell in it, had the impression of flying straight as an arrow, both feet off the forest floor, toward the iron frame that held the cooking pots suspended in his outdoor home. Pigtails didn't love me. It was true. I returned to the farmhouse on the Somerset Levels with its wonky kitchen and uneven floor and unfair advantage and said goodbye to the dog. I packed my bags. I don't remember the goodbye. He was probably whining on about *unconditional love*. Still itching, still with hurt snaking from ankle to hip, I drove my pink camper to a cottage buried deep in a dripping wood where a folk band lived who were kind, who I knew, who let me stay. In their bathroom I cut off my hair with kitchen scissors, and with a razor shaved it down to the skin. When I looked in the mirror I cried. In the sitting room was a crowd making plans for a Rainbow Gathering. They had a coach like the ones used for school trips to Box Hill, thirty children racing for the back row, someone being sick only this one had all the seats ripped out and sofas put in. Curtains were hung on the many windows; a kitchen had been installed and there were no children or anyone racing anywhere. There was a bed, large and messy, where me and my agonised spine and shaved head were installed as we waved goodbye to the folk band friends, the cottage in the dripping wood and set off for Czechoslovakia.

20

A CONNECTION WITH CZECHOSLOVAKIA

There was a connection with Czechoslovakia that I didn't think of as I set off in that coach, a shaved head, a disc slipping. In the tall, cold house in London where I'd grown up, we'd had a nanny, a refugee from the revolution, the Prague Spring that was crushed by the Russians. My mother had taken many people in and this nanny was one of them, she was given the flat in the basement and the job of looking after us. She had curly red hair, and she was traumatised though I knew her as frightening which was why as I set off on that coach for a Rainbow Gathering in the Gratzen Mountains, the seats replaced with armchairs, a bed at the back, I didn't think of her. I had shut her, and the crazed rampage of her, out of my mind. But everything is connected. We got the ferry to France, drove up the coast to Holland, stopped in a park in Amsterdam where my friends went out for the night and I stayed on the coach smoking pot. A man peered in at the many windows, circling. I huddled on the bed growing frightened, scenarios of rape and death ripping through my mind. I knew if he boarded the coach I'd be trapped. Something took me over. I went to the front, opened the door. Outrage at his imposition had made me wild. I doubled in size. I screamed fury at him, threw all the knives in my heart. He backed away and was swallowed by the night. I went back to bed. My friends returned. Somewhere in Germany a dawn filled with birds had us piled on the dirt road stretching from travel. I hung off the door frame to straighten my spine and bent on my knees to a tree seeing god in a halo of light. In the wooded mountains of Czechoslovakia we parked in a clearing, took acid and walked the last few kilometres of sandy road, collecting others as we went, this amassing of bare feet and blankets, dreadlocks and staffs to a place of tipis and fire and incessant drumming. Smoke curled into blue sky. I watched it circle the camp, giant and white above us, a snake, its mouth open, eating its tail.

21

LIKE THE THIRD EYE
IN A SKULL

I don't remember much because my disc was slipping. Because I was out of my mind in pain. Rainbow Gatherings are surreal places at the best of times, an army of people who believe in walking, they collect around the world in barefoot harmony, moved by a prophesy that the People of the Rainbow will make war go away. Everything is shared, there's a sense of life simplified, a medieval camping trip without the toothache. There are no nations or nationalities, only feathered hippies, their children on their hips, scant possessions fashioned onto homemade toolbelts, a tin cup and wooden utensil, a knife stuffed down the back of loose trousers, a staff you've carved yourself, beads swapped for tobacco. That's the look and premise, anyway, although try separating a Rainbow Warrior from his special stick if you want to see something nearer the truth. Humans are humans the world over. There was a lot of purposeful striding across soft grassland, tipi doors thrown open, shawls readjusted and elders muttering in private circles. A sense of a bunch of people trying to find something more important to talk about other than how sick they were of beans. There was a lot of bowing. And nakedness. Each day an enormous circle was formed of anyone hungry, volunteers ladled offerings into bowls held aloft. More beans. There was a lot of drumming. I teamed up with the renegades who'd made a camp of their own in the woods. Fewer prayers. Less sincerity. I remember the devilishly handsome Frenchman who took Datura and lost his mind, fell in a river and died. I remember the full moon appearing like the third eye in a skull. I'd made it into a tent when the disc between my fourth and fifth vertebrae gave up its efforts like the appendix and fallopian tube before it. When a sound came out of my mouth that I didn't recognise, I thought I was channelling a demon. But it must have been screaming because three women amassed like angels above me, then the face of someone I knew. A friend from the West Country, who one day would die but not that day, appeared out of nowhere. I didn't know he was there. He gathered me in his arms and carried me to France, to the house I'd trashed when I was fresh out of school, where my parents were on holiday. We arrived dirty from the road, unexpected and unannounced. Amongst palm trees and clean sheets, he laid me down.

22

MY HANDSOME AND KIND
KNIGHTS TEMPLAR

The house in France was a haven and still is. It sits on a crystal mountain on the edge of a national park, its walls hold a peace and a sanctuary. It's where my parents spent time together without one of them disappearing off to his studio and the other packing her car on a Sunday night. There were guests, but they were nice, the rooms were broad and warm, the garden messy and secret, at night wild boars came snouting about the roses. As a child I'd play on the drive with my busybody men mending potholes. I learnt to swim in the pool, I smoked my first cigarette, stolen from a packet left out on the terrace, in an airless, windowless bathroom. My father who died sixteen years ago is there; his presence as crystal clear as the mountain. I see him in the hall in soft hat and pink shirt, off for coffee in the village, or on the roof mending tiles, the scent of lemon trees and E45, happy in the sunshine. That summer he padded about not getting involved with the catastrophe that was me. My mother in lilac Liberty shirt fawned over my handsome and kind Knights Templar who had carried me across Europe in his arms. She was delighted by him while I lay on a sunlounger, shaved head, a painful buddha. She called a doctor who laid me on my front and lifted my leg till I screamed and hit him. He agreed the disc had ruptured, there were pieces floating in spinal fluid, and returned with a huge needle. The muscle relaxant, pierced into the flesh of my backside, made me scream again but after he'd gone, I went outside and sank into the pool, the weightlessness of water. The summer passed, croissant and Paris Match, tomatoes from the garden, my mother in lilac Liberty shirt, my father on the roof. Departure came like autumn. My father disappeared in his Porsche. My mother packed the car. We dropped my handsome and kind Knights Templar off on the motorway to hitchhike to Spain to see his children. My mother put on her tape of Anna Karenina. I reclined in the front seat to save my pain. Avignon and Lyon whipped past. Supine in the low-slung Citroën, I watched the sky and imagined Russian farming, Count Vronsky in the snow, Anna in her red coat as we reached Dover, the ferry to England and home.

23

A TALL, COLD HOUSE
IN LONDON

Home to the tall, cold house in London, my ruptured disc and I, this place of my childhood where Hollywood stars lit cigarettes with survivors of Russian oppression, where refugees and royalty passed each other on the stairs. Or used to. As a child, my father's friends and my mother's politics built a world of artists and argument. My father was Scottish aristocracy, a Tory-voting, Maggie-loving, patron of the arts. My mother was a member of the Labour Party who liked to pretend to be in touch with the real world while keeping a horse in the country. Why they married is a mystery I've lately been unravelling, they seemed so ill-disposed to suit each other. They had parallel lives, joined by artistic intellect, separated by their need to live exactly as they chose; she in the tall, cold house in London giving refuge to the lost and the lonely, he in a small, low-beamed cottage in Sussex. Both homes were part of vast estates he'd inherited and bought, a fact she bore with something close to shame. He wanted a wife who enjoyed tea with the Queen.

I'm not sure what she wanted, not him, anyway. He'd come up to town occasionally and they'd meet like their guests on the stairs, one coming down for a Cinzano before supper, the other rushing up to get changed for a meeting. She was an architect; he was a writer. Her drawings dominated the dining room table where we never ate while in the kitchen where we did, my father in bow tie and three-piece suit, would crouch at the end with his tea or drink, about to go out, never staying. We had a housekeeper who made marmalade and hated everyone except for my father and us and a fat, funny artist who lived downstairs and painted and never sold. There was the woman from Czechoslovakia in the basement flat. Amongst these ever-moving feet I found my place in Lego, my cat, my teddy. A house of parallel realities; the need and the glamour upstairs and in the basement flat, something else. But in 1995, I only knew that I was cold and my back was broken. The surgeon said it was lucky I was young, he wouldn't fuse the vertebrae, L4 and L5 would remain as independent as my parents. He removed the floating bits of disc and sowed me up and sent me to lie on the sofa and stare at the paintings that hung on the dining room walls; Inveraray Castle where my grandmother had grown up, the 8th Duke of Argyll bearing down over snapshots of us.

24

RETURN TO THE SOURCE

Retrieving my van from the dripping wood where I'd left it to go to Czechoslovakia, I returned to Latimer Road in West London, the house in which I'd lived before my detour to Glastonbury and snare in a ménage à trois. It was a time of parties and protests, MDMA and Reclaim The Streets, me and my split-screen camper with its twenty-one windows and a roof that slid back, a miniature sink and tiny plug under the bed, I named her Hera. In Hera I drove to derelict buildings behind King's Cross taken over by techno, to squatted land in Wandsworth turned into a riverside farm. A girl who'd been sectioned in Hackney Marsh got us on a mission to that place of stopped clocks to rescue her. We danced to a broken strip light in the lift and spirited her out hidden under a blanket in the back. On Battersea Bridge we held up traffic and graffitied the tarmac, put on a party til the police shut us down. We took a lot of psychedelics. We laughed. Our friends had a club called Return To The Source, a psychedelic trance night born of Space Tribe that came to life at The Rocket in Holloway and south of the river at The Brixton Academy. We decorated and danced; London was turned beautiful in the morning light. At the New Year's Eve party in Brixton I was deep in the wild when the bodies parted on the dance floor like the Red Sea and at the end of this pulsing human tunnel stood the man whose back I had leaned against in the Moroccan tent at the Harvest Fair that summer when two hundred people had taken off on a psilocybin spaceship and spun around the universe. He saw me and I saw him. He was six foot seven and had the face of an angel. We laughed and hugged and recognised, let go and got on with the night. I wore spandex flares covered in moon and stars bought from Anjuna market. My hair was still short but I would make it shorter. It was our second coinciding, there'd be a third before he and I decided there was something, before I set off on a personal mission to get him, shaving my head again. Pursuing him felt like a challenge I couldn't turn away from, a man with the face of an angel who'd been celibate for seven years. A red rag to my injured bull. He told me he had a thing for Sinéad O'Connor.

25

THE KEY

I was living in a squat in Ealing when the key came through the door. Hang on. Let's roll back a bit. The sea of bodies parted, he was six foot seven and had the face of an angel, we hugged hello and maybe we hung out a bit on that pulsing psychedelic dance floor and then we went our separate ways. The next time we met was by firelight in the woods near Newbury where a camp was set up to protest the building of a bypass. People were living up trees and refusing to come down, I'd driven out in my camper to join the fight. It was night, dark, mud and dirty faces. I parked and approached the first circle of flickering warmth and there he was on the other side. This third meeting proved too much for both of us. Fate, we agreed, was at play. I was determined, he was hesitant. He'd had other plans involving Sinéad O'Connor. I shaved my head again to look more like her. It did the trick. He took me to see the rhododendrons bloom in Windsor Great Park. We listened to Mike Scott and The Waterboys. I met his friends. He was in a band, he lived in a squat in Ealing, a two-hundred-year-old factory of bricked-up doors, freezing water, a maze of narrow stairs. I moved in and signed up at a music school thinking maybe this is it, this other thing I've been searching for. I sang a bit and was bad at it and shivered in the rigged-up shower cubicle and smoked spliffs at the rickety kitchen table picked up from a skip and one day a key came through the door. Hold on a minute. How did they find me, these people who sent it? It was a squat, right? Nobody knew I was there; I hadn't told my parents as I'd moved and moved and moved again. Yet there it was, a large brown envelope heavy with a key which slipped out onto my lap. The factory was quiet, my friends all sleeping, my boyfriend, that six-foot-seven angel quiet in our basement room and I was alone at the rickety kitchen table. I pulled out the letter that came with it, a letterhead I knew. The lawyers who handled my father's affairs by extension handled mine. It said, *Dear Eleanor, your house is between tenants, would you like to come and see it?* The key was fairy tale, huge and heavy, iron and rusted, teeth to fit an ancient lock. Had I told my friends that squatting wasn't my only option? Did they know I had money? I put the letter away and turned the key over in my hands.

26

A DAY OUT WITH
MY FATHER

I don't think I'd told my friends I was the kind of girl who got keys through the post from law firms in Westminster about houses that were empty and mine, but they took it in their stride. As we piled into my camper, my tall and pretty as an angel boyfriend, his dog, some of the band, a few friends who'd been passing by I remembered the last time I'd been there. It had been a day like that one, sunny and bright, summer coming. I was eleven years old; I'd been hanging about in the low-beamed kitchen of the cottage where my father lived, the place we invaded at weekends. 70's jeans, Kickers on my feet, my mother baking bread and my father in tweed suit and wellies saying, *Come along. I'm taking you to see your house.* His Porsche on the gravel, the soft front seat, his ordered hands on the wheel, the secure warmth of him, it wasn't the *your house* that I registered, it was the being with him; we could have driven in circles all day and I would have been happy. We slipped along narrow sunken lanes, hedgerows green and stretching, the sun shining, the car warm and purring to a house on a hill hugged by woodland where a man tidied away the blankets he'd slept on in front of the wide fire, guarding the place while it was empty. I remember standing on the first floor and looking through the windows at the view stretching like the Serengeti. And now this same view, my rag-taggle friends and I, a pink camper, a black and white dog, the same sunshine, the same woods that hugged, the same expanse of fields and trees swooping. The key was turned in the lock, the ancient doors swung open, my friends disappeared into rooms, up stairs, calling out, opening windows. I sat on a low wall, remembering. The letter had said *between tenants* but what was to stop me? Nothing but a few parties to raise money to build the studio in the garden that my boyfriend and his band had always wanted. I touched the iron gate hitch shaped like Aries horns and decided. By the time we were on the road back to London, The House of Grow was born. Parties were about to happen. I wrote to those lawyers in Westminster and told them I was moving in.

27

HOUSE OF GROW

The queue snaked round the block hidden by traveller's vans. It was fifty pence on the door, up stairs so narrow you had to pass sideways. At the top, a bar fashioned out of a plank of wood across a doorway, behind us coats were thrown onto a mattress on the floor. We sold cheese and gave away booze to get around the licensing laws. The mushroom tea was free, ladled into plastic cups from a vast, hot vat; harvested ourselves from the fields we hadn't bothered to pick out the grass and mud, England floated and sank amongst psychedelia. Nobody cared. Each room of that two-hundred-year-old factory was painted into its own party; a brick dungeon of techno, a psychedelic of trance, and deep in the belly through a maze of corridors a womb dressed in red velvet, where live cello made grown men weep. The building sweated and shook, through boarded-up doors steam escaped into the night. I remember thinking if fire ignites or a staircase collapses, none of us are getting out but nothing bad happened; no blaze or crush, week after week the wildness contained in a pulsing building in Ealing, the House of Grow parties to raise money for a studio in the country. Everyone was welcome. We turned no one away no matter what they did, like Mick who was huge, an overhung forehead, sunken eyes. He liked crack and scaring hippies and pissing in the womb but Bach and poetry brought him to his knees and he'd tell us about his mother. The police left us alone. They said the streets of Ealing were quieter when we were around. We took care of all the lost boys and girls. We had five of these parties I think, it's hard to remember because I was high and wild and dancing and serving mushroom tea and there is no record. On the day of the last one my angel-faced boyfriend discovered all the money we'd raised, that he'd stashed in a box, had been stolen. We didn't ask who did it. We went ahead anyway with the last party, a stomping, sweating, wild affair and then we left that factory in Ealing and drove to a farm in the country.

28

A LEAP OF FAITH

But first I jumped naked off a viaduct in Normandy. Almost naked. We'd driven in convoy, Angel man and me, to a festival in northern France where there were more crew than punters and we lay about in the sunshine smoking pot and he said, *Let's go bungee jumping.* It was appropriate, that leap into nothing, trusting a rope I couldn't see and trusting the calculations of others who said if I reached out my hand, I would touch the water in that microsecond halt between going down and bouncing up. A leap of faith echoed in the leap to leave the squat in Ealing and move to a farmhouse high up on a hill hugged by woodland. I don't know why I elected to strip, just me and a pair of tiny pink shorts flying from a bridge. Probably showing off. It made sense at the time. I remember Angel man rushing up to do it again and almost jumping before they'd attached the chord. I remember someone doing it on a bicycle. I remember the ridiculous rush of stepping into nothing, my brain telling me I would die. It was a rush to catch the ferry too, that afternoon, we were late, we'd picked up new friends, we had various drugs to hide as we sped to the border. I was so blasé. Being caught – and we never were – never crossed my mind. We ruled the world. It was all about friends, new connections, wherever we went we made them. Two more that weekend who came with us back to the farm. We set them to work stripping carpets and scrubbing underlay, revealing wide floorboards. This house in the country that I owned, to which I'd been sent an ancient key had ancient stone and brick and oak hidden beneath wall-to-wall sixties interior; beige cupboards, avocado carpets and red plastic lino gave way to stone and oak and brick. Everybody worked for free and a piece of what we were building, a scene in a house in the country, wisteria dripping, sun shining, kettle always on. We filled the bedrooms with mattresses pulled from skips and filled them with people. We tore and painted and smoked and practised circus skills in the garden. Everyone was learning to juggle. Acrobalance was all the rage. We decided to start a commune.

29

HOW TO START A COMMUNE

Let me set the scene. Me and Angel man. A carpenter who looked like Jesus. A pianist, blonde, many rings, she played the Michael Nyman tune from *The Piano* almost constantly. A man of the woods and his Wiccan wife and her daughter. An ex-trucker turned megalithic giant. A soft-spoken road protester who'd lived up a tree. A long, thin, angular beanpole with glasses. An old man and white-haired woman, both of them rounded like the bender they built in the wood. These were the first members of the commune. God did people go on about how great communal living would be. That's why we did it. That's why when I looked out on the land, I said, *Well let's find out then, shall we.* A pound a week, everyone welcome, an open-door policy, communal use of the washing machine and bathrooms, you could pitch up and pitch anywhere, the house soon full, tipis, benders, yurts sprang to life in the woods and fields. Converted horseboxes found flat ground outside the old metal barn down the drive where a mechanic had been turfed out. A member of the firm behind all this, my father's estate, had arrived looking worried in a suit, clearly instructed to do my bidding, no questions asked, and he did; we wanted the barn for ourselves. It was big enough for workshops and later a stage and trapeze. The road protester moved his coffin onto a shelf in the office. The megalithic giant announced the HQ for Shamanic Studies. The Jesus carpenter hammered and plane-sawed and got dust in his beard. A didgeridoo maker portioned off another corner, soon discovering that giant hogweed was no replacement for eucalyptus. Meetings once a week, mandatory, a talking stick passing from hand to hand around the kitchen table. A lot of tea. A lot of spliff. In the first month we sent out a call for extra help, gave everyone a sapling and an ecstasy. We planted two thousand trees that day. Word spread, the commune grew and this wasn't the wildness of Dartmoor or some remote hilltop in the highlands where no one could see, it was Surrey, the Home Counties, not two hours from London where careful women clipped their roses and nervous men played golf.

30

LET'S BUILD A STONE
CIRCLE BY HAND

They came in droves, the druids, led by ex-trucker turned megalithic giant, Ivan McBeth. He was the friend from Longleat who'd opened my eyes to the fuckery of the man with pigtails. Next time you're at Glastonbury Festival, go to the Swan Circle. He built it. His ghost roams those stones amongst the people off their heads, his ashes are scattered there. When I'd arrived at the farm, I'd looked from the kitchen window at a flat jut of land on the hillside and rung him. I'd said, *Let's build a stone circle by hand,* knowing he'd never done it, knowing every build before had been with forklift trucks and cherry pickers, and how much he wanted to feel the rough warm haul of his ancestors. One sentence and he came. Shamanic HQ was set up in the metal barn, the megalithic call was sent out. Ovates, bards and druids, they called themselves Club Meg; the keepers of the ancient sites, from Cornwall to Callanish. And with them came the others, the Wiccans and Pagans and hippies and people of the woods, sacred geomancers, engineers, those who knew what they were doing and those who really didn't, travellers and runaways, the brilliant and lonely; we welcomed them all. Word spread. The land filled with benders, yurts, trucks and tipis. The carpenter climbed to the top of a sequoia and fixed a chair, it's still there if you're brave enough to see. And as the land filled and the seasons changed Ivan watched the rise and fall of the moon and plotted its course across the sky. By May he was ready, the stones found in a quarry in Portland and delivered to the site by truck, dumped in an unceremonious pile, eighteen nine-ton rocks which became nineteen when one in its crashing course from the tipped-up flatbed broke in half. We would begin the build with a festival, Beltane, when bluebells covered the forest floor. A hot tub was built, erected on stalks like a rocket about to take off. A huge and comfortable yurt would hold our meetings, a communal kitchen would feed us, we were a megalithic village appearing on a Surrey hillside; dogs, children, sunshine, the neighbours in sensible shoes came and gawped. But Beltane was coming, and we were full of fire, and Kings would race naked and a Queen would be crowned and the first of the stones would go in.

31

THE MAY QUEEN

This post is dedicated to Lourdes, who we loved. I can name her because of what happened, but it doesn't happen yet. I have a photograph of her in her finery, dancing round the maypole in a blue satin dress, her arm raised in song moments before she met her king, the carpenter who dances behind her. She was Portuguese, Wiccan, dark curls, silk voice. She appeared in the commune that Beltane as the village rose on the hill and the stones were delivered; I don't remember whose friend she was, who brought her, how she found us, but that year the women of the camp crowned her May Queen. It was she who sat on the throne by the Beltane fire, a wreath of ivy in her hair as the men stripped and trotted away, the carpenter taking off his hat, a crowd of male nakedness disappearing into the woods. They climbed to the top of the hill scaring dog walkers and waited for the bellow of the horn. We were gathered, hundreds of us, dressed in skins and rags and finery, the stones still a pile of rocks in the sequoia trees, as the animal call rang out and the naked men ran. Crashing through undergrowth, ignoring paths, straight down the hill, we heard them before we saw them. The hollering of ancient fire and beast, a camp of dancing Pagans on a sunny Surrey hillside in May calling them in with drums beating, flames leaping, the neighbours alerted by smoke and cries came hesitantly up the drive. Our megalithic giant in velvet top hat and loincloth raised his hands to blue sky while muddy children chased dogs and women skipped about with flowers in their hair. And there, suddenly, the naked men streamed from the wood, a terrifying leap of barbed wire and they were in the field, hurtling across grassland to be the first, to claim the Beltane Queen as their own. The carpenter won her, was crowned May King, and together they leapt the fire; she was his for a year. Tradition had it he would lose his head to the next king the next year but he lost his head to her instead. They fell in love and were joined for more than a year and it wasn't him who died – but not yet. Five hundred pagans on a hill, we raised a maypole, we raised the first King and Queen and then we raised the first stone.

32

HOW WE LEARNT TO
MOVE ROCKS

This is how we did it. Telegraph poles and railway sleepers, an engineer taught us how to use a windlass; a rope looped around a stone and a tree, and tightened with a stick turned clockwise, a coordination of hands to keep it winding and stop it snapping out of control and spinning anticlockwise; an arm was broken once, and once the rope broke and whipped me. But first we had to lever each stone from the pile. We used wooden poles to inch our way under, another pole, bigger and so on, inch by inch we lifted those stones onto telegraph poles placed crossways on sleepers that led to a hole in the ground at least half as deep as each stone was tall so that when it fell it would not be moving again except by rabbits who nibble and tip in that quiet way that builds mountains and digs canyons. A hundred people on a rope, rocks hauled along tracks, a bridge built across grass for a Portland stone to float towards a spot chosen by our Megalithic Giant that would mark a rise of the moon. Five hundred people on a hill for a month, living on campfire cooking and starting each day with The Dance of Life. Meetings – oh god the meetings. A talking stick, an endless circle of discussion from who isn't doing the washing up to which stone cares that it broke in half. We had to hold a ceremony for that. The Megalithic Giant convinced us to let him try levitation. It didn't work but we had fun. Uri Geller got in touch, invited us to his house of obscene crystals and damn spoons and boasted he'd magic the stones into place but guess what never turned up. It wasn't the showmen who got those stones moved but the engineers who spoke quietly, who knew that no fancy trickery is going to get around the moment when a nine-ton rock reaches a hole in the ground and falls in. If it lands at an angle that's it. You can move a stone across grass but it takes more than an armful of chanting Pagans to push a rock vertical that has landed at a slant. You can't do it. As each stone fell, we held our breath, as each landed perfectly we cheered and the tamping sticks moved in, and the didgeridoos played and the drums beat and beneath each stone is buried something to make each of us who were there smile and tease the archaeologists of a thousand years from now.

33

SOMEWHERE IN ALL
OF THIS

L et me expand because we were a village of misfits and outcasts, a tribe of off-grid outer-reaches travellers with an open-door policy that attracted the lost and the lonely as much as the brilliant and brave. We were unruly, anarchic, we somehow governed each other and ourselves. Healers, musicians, mystics, those who made sure the shit pits were dug, others who prayed and cried. Bodgers and woofers got stuck in with fences and fires, party people decorated trees, foragers taught us what to eat. The traumatised and frail, turned out by psychiatric care, they came too and spoke in tongues and claimed to be Jesus, others channelled messages from Angels and Aztecs; my actual Angel man and I accepted them all. People got together, babies were born, the commune grew. There were children and dogs everywhere. Mud beneath our nails, the kettle always on. As word spread that we were building a stone circle by hand another layer of engineers and mystics was added, those who'd made it their life's work to understand the majesty of how and why. More benders and yurts sprang up in the woods, the metal barn expanded, Shamanic Studies HQ was busy with the ringing of the phone while the seasoned road protester slept in a coffin on a shelf and ate oats and was as gentle as a branch waving. A stage was built, a trapeze hung, for each of the eight pagan festivals we held a party, druids everywhere, and on the last weekend of every month we raised another stone. Unlike Uri Geller who'd invited us to his house to admire his crystals and bent spoons, who'd showed us his car but when it came to it never showed up, hundreds of others did. Keepers of stone circles from all over Britain found their way to us. Ed Pryn with his flowing robes, white hair and bottle glasses, John and Elizabeth, keepers of Callanish in the Hebrides, John Michell, author of *How the World Is Made: The Story of Creation According to Sacred Geometry* who quietly put his hand to a rope. When notices from the council arrived, challenging our right to build the circle, a man who I'd known as just another face around the fire, revealed himself to be Someone High Up in local politics. He showed us how to navigate our way through the attempts to stop us. He saved us. And somewhere in all of this I flew to Sedona in Arizona, that place of vortexes and portals, and trained to be a yoga teacher.

34

A TROUBLE IN MY BONES

I spent a month in the desert of Sedona training to be a yoga teacher. I hung out with a man and his guitar singing songs that sounded like *Paris, Texas*. I hitched a ride in a camper and drove down through Utah and New Mexico where the rocks are piled like coins. I met an old friend and got hit by a truck on the highway, nearly turning us over. I flew home with yoga fitness to a commune thriving with musicians and healers, my Angel man waiting, a recording studio built in a cabin in the garden, his band rehearsing. Bali happened too, somewhere in all this, a storm on a boat, almost shipwrecked, washing me up on the shores of Komodo. I knelt at a tree and gave thanks and ate rice and stood on a table watching dragons. I was searching, and at home I searched too. Healers laid me on grass, ran their hands through the air and told me I was this or that; it was past life trauma, a trapped soul, a possession, a hex, an entity, darkness – an opinion on each other's pain was easy. We tore down a barn to release a trapped soul murdered there. We circled the house in crystals and stayed up all night with a crying ghost baby in a bedroom. We cleansed and wafted and chanted and lit, we rebirthed and trailed sage and clouds of glory. We prayed and meditated and channelled and explained. Everyone was on the candida diet. Angel man and I did Vipassana, ten days' silent retreat in Wales and returned light as air but the meditation had frightened me, the sitting had felt like free falling and I'd written a poem on my pillow with a contraband pencil found under the mat of my room. Gong baths, didge healing, Bowen therapy, I did everything yet still the feeling persisted, what happened, a search for an answer that would answer the sense of disquiet. I had been sad all my life. I had retreated and felt alone. And the stones went up one by one and the year swung round and the disquiet persisted, a trouble in my bones, but it would be put aside temporarily, this search, because coming down the tracks was a wedding.

35

THE PROPOSAL

We used to hang out at the Bonnington Café in Vauxhall, but he didn't propose to me there. He chose a farm trailer parked by the metal barn, straw bales against my back. He'd written a song and I didn't see it coming. He was always singing something, devoted to his band, they wanted to make it big. My six-foot-seven Angel man; when we'd moved into the farm, I'd gone out to an architectural salvage to find a bath long enough. The piano player had painted clouds in a blue sky on the ceiling of our bathroom, the carpenter had built a plinth, a little spiral of steps, a German couple, obsessed with twelve egg omelettes, had done the plumbing and I probably went there, to that enormous, high-up bath after the proposal, I probably sought out the comfort of water because I shouldn't have said yes. He took me by the hand and said, *I want to play you something,* and he was nervous, I could tell and it wasn't like him to be afraid. He led me to the trailer, settled me against the bales of straw and took up his guitar that was already there, prepared for the moment he'd planned. I listened to the words and then I heard them and then I said yes because he was so gentle and it was so sweet and I was frightened for his heart, how I would hurt it if he didn't put it back in his chest right now, so I said yes but I shouldn't have. I should have said, *Wait, let me think about it.* He will be reading this and he will disagree, he will say it was perfect, what happened, it had to happen like that and while that's true, it's also true that I shouldn't have said yes because the inside of me didn't match the outside and I was yet to learn how important that is. So while the sun shone and I made all the moves of happy, on the inside clouds were gathering and I thought, *What have I done?* I knew I'd been proposed to, and I knew he was a good man and he loved me and had not a bad bone in his body. And I knew my friends were shocked because when we held a party at the Bonnington Café to announce our news one of them screamed and covered her mouth.

36

THE BUILD-UP

Yesterday a package arrived from my brother's office, a file of things my father had kept, the notice of my birth, letters from me to him, addresses of all the places I have lived from Zimbabwe to Australia, and among it all was the newspaper article about my wedding in the woods. That's what happens when you open cupboards, all this stuff flies out, brothers, without warning, send you packages they meant to send you years ago but forgot. That's when you know you're onto something. We announced the wedding at the Bonnington Café and pandemonium broke out which in hippie speak means we sat around smoking spliffs and dreaming big. A hand fasting. A three-day party. I would ride side-saddle. His band would play. The commune set to clearing a place high up in the forest that gave a small platform of flat; it was thick with bracken, it was where the biggest sequoias grew, still grow, I stood there yesterday and remembered. It's a sea of dense green again now and the altar has crumbled, just a stone sticking up like a lighthouse if you know where to look, but twenty-six years ago four hundred people gathered there in all their finery, ribbons and an altar and a horse and you and me; you in a suit made from your granny's curtains and me with silk butterflies tied between my toes. We planned everything, how your granny would be carried in a litter built by the carpenter, how I would ride side-saddle through the woods dressed in white. You invited everyone. Friendly chats stopped at traffic lights resulted in invitations being passed out of windows. Your best friend and guitarist from the band was to be best man. And this is why I must tell it in parts, just a little today, the build-up, the dreams, and tomorrow what happened because no matter what we planned other plans were happening too. While I learnt to ride side-saddle on my mother's horse, rehearsing the balance, you rehearsed the songs you would sing to me and he rehearsed something else, he must have, it was so orchestrated. And the energy built and the sequoias towered and the band practised and I know why this is so hard to write, and so do you.

37

THE WEDDING

It's true, I rode side-saddle, barefoot, silk butterflies tied to my toes, glass jewels about my eyes, a white slip hemmed with pearls and roses, a Victorian veil, a crown of flowers, nine maidens. Our guests divided, the women with me, the men with you to the wedding circle high on the hill. Flautists in the trees, drummers on the path, gongs hanging from branches made echo in the wind, a late-summer, warm September day in Surrey, a stone circle half built. My father and mother waiting for me in an archway, he, eccentric, loving it, she, moved and likely worried, the rest of my family dispersed amongst guests amused, probably, the latest ridiculousness, what next, this, a pagan wedding in the woods. We walked the ribbons, you and I; yellow and blue, I the sun and you the moon, your dog running, me on the arm of my father, he wore a tweed suit and wellies, a pheasant feather stuck in a deerstalker hat. My veil trailed over the woodland floor, snagging on brambles, the maidens blew bubbles, our audience of guests, propped on fallen logs, watched a choreographed ceremony of us. A Megalithic

Giant and a Dakini goddess to bind us, the altar a tower of stone and twist of candles, clouded in incense and not yet broken. We read vows, swapped rings and were married. I didn't notice that your best man wasn't there. There was so much cheering. We descended together through the woods to the party at the farmhouse; champagne, food and speeches, you sang on stage, we partied all night but the next day there would be a phone call which you took quietly. You gathered me up, back to the wedding circle, I remember twelve of us sitting where you and I had married, you said you had something to say. Your best man's wife had rung. At the hour you and I were married when he should have been there, he had instead dressed in his full regalia, placed his ceremonial knives about him, sent his wife out for orange juice and milk and taken his own life. He left her, his twelve-year-old son and baby daughter. He left you. And I remember thinking, *You should have told me first.* I knew then it was over before we'd begun. I know now what shock does.

38

THE HONEYMOON

Shall we take a breath? Because it's hard, this memoir business, and what happened yesterday and twenty-six years ago, was painful. A man died on my wedding day and we never talked about it, Angel man and me, at least I don't remember we did, not how I would now when something scarring like that happens. I know we were in shock but we were also young and without the tools and wherewithal to understand that taking a breath is vital. Without it, it's impossible to know where to go next, without it one just stumbles on which is what we did, to Mull. But wait, before we go, I want to say this; that writing a memoir is like pulling out thorns one by one. I didn't know it when I began – like starting a commune or building a stone circle or getting married in a wood, I started by accident of idea unthought out yet every morning I wake at four and I write and thorns work their way to the surface. All sorts of friends have come forward to lend a hand and pliers; yesterday the Dakini goddess wrote to say how angry she was at the time when she heard of his death and it was another thorn removed.

I had never heard her say that. But a man died leaving a wife and two children and they deserved more than an announcement in a wood, a pain unspoken, a party carried on; I didn't know that my new husband was crushed by the grief inside, he had such a gift for holding everything lightly I mistook it for not caring. I didn't know how to take a breath but I am taking one now. It was terrible. I have cried. Yet twenty-six years ago we headed off on honeymoon to Mull, to the house of a friend who told me yesterday he'd missed our wedding on strict instructions from another friend to get the house ready for us, sorry about that, and we spent ten days or so up there in that beautiful place, Scotland in my blood, but I don't remember much. I remember the train journey. I remember sitting on opposite sides of the carriage. I remember not speaking.

39

THE AFTERMATH

Remember the girl we sprang from Hackney Marsh psychiatric unit where we danced to the broken strip light in the lift? We returned from Scotland to a chaos expressed by her – pyramids of used teabags all over the fields, and in the house, wedged into corners, teddy bears facing mirrors. She'd broken down. My man disappeared into Vispassana, meditating twice a day but I had no faith. And the stones went in, one by one, heaving their way toward completion through winter into spring. As the circle came together the commune fell apart, dividing into factions which fought and bitched. The metal barn complained that the house thought they were special. Those in the house said the metal barn lot were unfriendly. The tipis, yurts and benders assumed they knew best. Arguments at weekly meetings, the talking stick travelling. Was it right to keep an owl, eat wheat, let anybody in, even the ones who'd gone mad. The pixie girl who'd broken down disappeared into the woods. Fruitarians arrived, their skin and hair a matching grey. Breatharians sneaked biscuits in the middle of the night. Too many women in the kitchen. A baby was born. The Portuguese Wiccan who had once been May Queen got thinner. Across the hill was another commune of sorts, not a hippy pagan one but a Christian evangelical one; a hill of Golgotha, a cave with a stone, a cross that an actor dragged over his shoulder once a year in a Passion Play that stretched four hours, brought thousands of devotees to another religion, a life of Christ played out in the Surrey hills. The Director asked if I'd like a job, he was gathering cast and crew, he needed a stage manager. I drove my pink camper out of the commune to his converted barn, clean and bright, a different piece of England a mile down the road where people wore shoes and worried about the shopping, where there were no loincloths except on stage, and there, in his kitchen, met Jesus.

40

THE PASSION

Not the real Jesus, obviously. The actor playing Jesus, and the effect he had was unholy. It was instant, that thing I didn't know I'd been missing. With the Director, who still makes me laugh to this day, I found a real friend and with Jesus I found something biblical. It fizzed. It was alive. From the moment we locked eyes. I remember walking into the Director's kitchen and thinking, *Shit*. These shows were no amateur productions, a cast of hundreds, an audience of thousands, the actors trail the story over a park dedicated to the spreading of the word and this Jesus had been playing the part for many years. He was well known and well loved and he was treated like the actual Jesus so the extra thrill when we'd come off set and drink wine in the Director's kitchen and try not to touch because I was married was crack to my devilish heart. Jesus also liked actual crack, a fact the Producers, who were very Christian indeed, drew a veil over. But he would go missing sometimes and I would stand in for him at rehearsals and tech runs, a cross dragged on my shoulder, a surreal afternoon spent crucified on the hill of Golgotha. I knew this about him and I didn't care, I too was an addict although I didn't know it. And I never once thought of the feelings of my husband at home and I couldn't wait to drive away from the commune which lumbered on, fractious and barefoot to the Director's house where Jesus waited. It was the distraction I'd been looking for. While my husband made music in the studio we'd built, his tall frame bent over the mixing desk his parents had given us for our wedding, I put on a tool belt and boots and discussed the logistics of rolling a stone from the mouth of a cave and how to walk on water. I didn't know the Producers knew who I was and what I did, where I came from, a stone circle near completion, the pagan soul of me. But they were watching, too. They were well aware of a heathen striding about their land with a walkie-talkie distracting their Jesus from his lines. When he disappeared the night before curtain up, they blamed me.

41

THE SACRIFICE

Because every good story needs a sacrifice and something lost. Jesus – devilish handsome, funny and sweet, an electricity coming off him like fire – god we'd had fun that summer, the sparks of something forbidden, an escape from a commune that had taken over and a marriage I hadn't meant to make. In the normality of the Director's house I laughed and ate ham and felt like just a girl. Jesus was my escape hatch and now he was missing. My husband at home – generous, majestic, kind, who loved me, who'd waited saying not a word while I'd gadded about without a thought in my head for him. And I didn't think of him that night either, the night before the show. I remember the lights being low in the Director's kitchen, it was dark outside when the Producers arrived, angry, not looking and looking at me. It had happened before, a missing Jesus, but before there'd been no heathen. Hurried conversations of which I was not a part, a car sent off to a den in Brixton. I went home. The next day I turned up on set, walkie-talkie and boots and so did he in robes and readiness for sacrifice and resurrection, chastised, head down, concentrating. I left him with the costume ladies and went to check props. The Producers in a Gator pulled up beside me. They told me to get off the land. Christianity was not happy. I returned to the commune, a stone circle almost built, a husband who knew, who called it before I did, had the guts I didn't. We had been married for less than a year. He suggested we end it with a trip, we took acid in the recording studio, *This Is Hardcore* powering from the speakers, my Angel man and I who wasn't mine anymore, who never had been, who I'd thrown over for a Christ with a wicked smile. There were endings coming, my marriage, the stone circle, a Wiccan life, the commune but Christianity wasn't done with me yet. First, they sent a priest and a mallet.

42

THE EXORCIST

We'd gutted a rabbit on the central stone the day Father Juniper came to exorcise the children. Blood and entrails smeared a rock. It didn't look great. We saw him lumbering up the field towards us, an enormous wooden crucifix over his shoulder. The hem of his brown robe was dampened by grass, his sandals snagged dandelions, his string of beads swung with every step. A squat woman followed dressed for weekend hiking; determined boots, no-nonsense shorts, furious hair. I want to give her a whistle and a map around her neck, though I'm not sure my memory isn't embellishing. But you get the picture. A low centre of gravity. Eyes looking for a fight. He wiped his brow and lent his cross against a stone. She took up a wide leg stance. "We've come to cast out the devil." The sun shone, it was a beautiful day, the stones were nearly finished, one lay on its side, a hole already dug. On such a day the view from the hill stretches to Chanctonbury Ring, The Weald a sea of green, it can look as if the last thousand years of people hasn't happened. Buzzards wheeled the sky, smoke drifted from the campfire, the hot tub like a rocket bubbled with children. There was a crowd of us gathered that weekend for the final stone, the yurts enormous and flapping, dogs grinning, pagans, engineers, hippies, Wiccans and druids many naked from the waist up smoked roll-ups, put the kettle on, washed cups. I'm sure we offered them tea before they got to work, and I'm sure they refused. I heard later that they'd gone to every house in the surrounding area, offering to bless and protect from the evil worship on the hill. In my neighbour's house a glass table had shattered when he'd walked in the door, and when we went to the wedding site, my soon-to-be ex-husband and I to say our goodbyes, we found that the altar had been smashed. My soon-to-be ex-husband. The end was coming. Tomorrow we'd put in the last stone.

43

THE LAST STONE

And all this time we'd been building a stone circle. Inch by inch over slow grass from pile to track to hole in the ground, the rise and fall of the moon marked in rock. A year and a bit, from Beltane to Summer Solstice, the last weekend of every month. In sunny weather crowds came, through winter hardly anyone at all. One wet and miserable December with only twelve of us up there we'd put in three stones because we'd got that good at it, because we'd learnt it was less about strength than coordination. And fewer people meant less chat. Over the building of the circle my marriage was born and broken. Jesus, who I saw one last disastrous time, had served his purpose, there was no relationship there either. My husband had said go and I had gone to London to meet him and find out what all this electricity was about but without the robes and forbidden touch there was nothing. I came home and the commune gathered and we orchestrated the end like the beginning. Beneath every stone were prayers and artefacts that meant something to us, and beneath the last stone we put our rings. I remember that day, standing at the brink together, the stone ready to tip, the Megalithic Giant beside us, others gathered about, Angel man and me, we took off our rings and earth covered them and the rock was heaved and fell and stood upright. That night we had a party, a full regalia dress-up, hundreds gathered to mark the completion of a stone circle built by hand, and the next day, or soon after, he left. He took the mixing desk and went to stay at my mother's. He sent an enormous television, delivered to the foot of my bed which felt like a recrimination. I remember the sudden void of him, how quickly I cried and just as quickly stopped, how the day felt simple. The stone circle was finished, the commune was three years settled with families, children were going to school, there was no reason to think it wouldn't carry on except now I was alone, no one to share it with. Did we fall apart after he left? Sort of. He was the only member of the commune who everyone loved. He unified us. It took a little time and someone coming down the line who would shatter all of it, but without him the fractious projective dogma grew stronger. And in the midst of it was a Wiccan woman in love with a carpenter who told us she knew what she was doing, and every day grew thinner.

44

LORDY DON'T LEAVE ME

There was a song we used to play, the words had her name in them, *Lordy don't leave me,* the Carpenter listened to it over and over. Her name was Lourdes, she'd arrived in our lives when the sun shone and everything was new, our first May Queen, she had black ringlet hair and the way she would say his name I can still hear now, the slant of a Portuguese accent, she seemed so knowledgeable. It was gradual, this eating less and less, small additions of things cut out, a concoction every morning that we called gretch; garlic, ginger, vinegar and oil, it was for cleansing the liver. We were all of us scrubbing at something. The farm was a revolving door of answers to the question of how to be happy, bloating was her devil, she brought the candida diet. When my husband left, she and the Carpenter left too, they moved into a house in Brighton. A friend saw her at a gig and it was the first time I heard someone say she was too thin. Not long after that, in the hall of her home, she collapsed and was carried by the man she loved to hospital where she died. Her organs had shut down. News reached the commune on a wave of anger, there was blame and talk of curses, her Wiccan circle decided she had higher intentions. Deaths explained with *this was their path* are easy to say once they've happened. When is it right to step in? What is the moment when your business becomes mine? She had starved herself to death right under our noses and what made me angry at the time and still does now is not that she chose to do this but that her trauma, acted out with food, was couched in an all-knowing wisdom. She was Wiccan and she was wise but she was also an addict and it killed her. We held meetings, her Wiccan friends came, the commune gathered, there was talk of burying her up at the stones, I made promises I couldn't keep, in the end we planted a tree which her man wrapped in barbed wire, no one could get near, a shrine to pain and her loss beside the newly finished stone circle. It was many years before he took the barbed wire away and we could breathe again. In hindsight it must have been this which made me go to London for a year. I can't have been in my right mind. I got it into my head that I wanted to be an actor and found my way to the only drama school in England, or perhaps the world, that turned out to be a cult.

45

DRAMA SCHOOL

It didn't say cult in the brochure. It said, *We will make you the best actor ever*, or some such shit because he was full of grand claims, the man who ran it. He's dead now, of a cancer that had any student brought to the table, he would have ridiculed and shamed. He was like that. He believed in breaking you down. He'd been trained through Est, a psychotherapy system that was watered down into The Landmark Forum but he knew it in its purest form. He had not an inch of kindness to him. Let me zero in on this word, cult. A Svengali leader. A place to belong that requires you cut off from the outside world. A doctrine that dictates *they* are fucked and you are saved. A requirement of absolute, unquestioning devotion. A list that grows of do's and don'ts, built by the leader's capricious whim. Mandatory daily rituals and punishments for failing. Cold baths every morning. Our hair a certain length, how we dressed dictated by him. If anyone ran away, they were fined £10,000 to come back which, crazy as it sounds, actually happened. If you walked down the corridor in a way he didn't like, or creased a piece of paper by the way you held it, he punished you with public ridicule and demands for money. He said to be someone else you had to think their thoughts and this was his excuse for the morning confession, the acting, drama school part of his tyranny, our chairs in a horseshoe around him, spilling in turn our darkest secrets about ourselves and others. He said our shame described us and that's the trouble with these things, the method of cults, because he did have truths which at first lit me up into thinking I'd found something brilliant. Wait. I have to stop here. I feel sick. I thought I could write this quickly because nothing in me wants to give this man and that place more than a page or minute more of my time, but I can't. I had forgotten how vulnerable I was to him. Like so much else I had buried it, filed it under *another funny story*. But now I'm looking I find I cannot pull it out in one shot. I am too angry.

46

A DAY IN THE LIFE
OF A CULT

That motherfucker. He smashed my brain. I'd moved to a flat in Tottenham with other students, a place we could watch our thoughts, police each other and go limp together. I would wake at five and make my packed lunch and drive to the freezing outdoor pool in Hampstead where I'd dive in and swim thirty lengths. At school by six, within a term the third years had given me the keys to open up the building, realising quickly they could get away with a lie-in. School began at seven with meditation, yoga, face exercises, eye exercises followed by the horseshoe of chairs around him. So far so good, right? Sounds healthy, all this cold water and stretching, that's the trouble with cults, there's often a grain of sense. He, Mr Svengali, wasn't wrong in thinking all those things helped a healthy mind, and nor that we are motivated by shame, that the psyche will do what it can to move away from pain and towards pleasure, that we've mostly been conditioned to hide. Breaking someone down is easy. Anyone can do that. It's the holding and putting back together with care that's the hard bit, the bit that matters. It's what you do with the pieces when they're all over the classroom floor. You don't kick them and laugh unless you want to cause a shattering. In the horseshoe of shame confessions he encouraged us to say what we thought of each other and ourselves, the more abusive the better. He told us to bring in baby photos so that he could rip into our earliest parts. He understood absolutely the power of language and used words to cut us open. He said, *Whow me your soft underbelly*, and then took out a knife. I won't use the words here. He doesn't deserve it. And if we'd gone out for the weekend into normal life, seen people not of the school, he'd make us admit it like a souring, a transgression that had set us back. We were ridiculed and shamed and fined and made to feel that only he could save us. And the acting bit? Yes, that happened, sort of, not much, we put on Russian plays, he told us relentlessly that we were lying. Day after day for a year, a dismantling in north London while my old life on the farm, the commune, carried on without me. Yesterday, when I finished the piece and pressed publish and was completely wrong-footed by the torrent, I found beneath my chair an old rusty nail, small, sharp and flat-headed. It was as if it had fallen out of me, the small, sharp poison that was him.

47

I AM COMING FOR YOU

I woke this morning with that Richard Wilbur quote spinning round my head – *Step off assuredly into the blank of your mind, something will come to you**. I have to remind myself that these are not a fluke, these daily posts that I get up and write every day. These episodes have been churning for decades. But here's the thing, it's only now when I string them together that they tell a story that I didn't know. They're no longer isolated fragments, they give context to each other. I didn't know quite how lost I was, how rudderless, how vulnerable to the intent of others nor how intent I was on finding answers. Although my father had his eye on me from afar and my mother in her own way cared, though they both loved me, they were absent. It was no wonder that I found myself in a cult, it's understandable that I was wide open to charlatans. From the charlatan who pretended to teach acting and liked to humiliate, a friend got me out. She came to see me. I said, *I'm so unhappy,* sitting on the counter in her kitchen, kicking my legs against the cupboards. She said, *You have to get out of there.* I returned to face the Svengali who'd discovered that day it was me who'd been opening the school every morning to give the third years a lie-in – a transgression that made him wild. I said, *I don't care; I'm leaving.* He said, *No one leaves, you'll be back,* but I knew I wouldn't. As I write this the lights in my kitchen keep flashing, an electrical short of the kind he would have ascribed to his powers, not the drama school man but the charlatan who came next, the boy from Kent who swam into the void left by drama school. Two years from the day I walked out of the cult this boy would vow a curse of a thousand years upon me, my family and the hill. He said that. Those were his actual words. He believed totally in his powers to frighten, as the cult leader had done. They were no different. One called himself the headmaster of a drama school. The other called himself Shaman. These people who think it their right to terrorise. I am coming for you.

As a Queen sits down, knowing that a chair will be there / Or a General raises his hand and is given field glasses / Step off assuredly into the blank of your mind / Something will come to you

48

THE EGG MAN COMETH

I had painted myself into a corner the day he arrived. Returned to the farm after a year away I no longer knew where I fitted into this thing we'd started, a commune in Surrey, everyone else getting on with it but I was lost. I'd set about my bedroom floor with white gloss, a fresh start, and forgotten to leave a way out. Barefoot, dripping paintbrush, my back against the wall, he appeared in the doorway and introduced himself. He didn't say, *I am the egg man,* but we came to know him as that. Many years ago when he was just a boy from Kent, he'd had a dream about a place in Mexico. Like it happens in the story books he'd taken a flight, walked into a cafe and a grizzled man had glanced from under a wide-brimmed hat and said, *I've been waiting for you.* He'd gone with this man, a shaman, into the jungle and emerged twelve years later a shaman also, whereupon he'd left his teacher and set up shop in India where a friend of mine met him and brought him back to the farm where he met me, dripping brush in hand, back against the wall, painted into a corner. His teacher had taught him the ways of divination by eggs;

a process of wafting and breathing and cracking into water, the white tendrils and yolk a replication of your innards, not just your guts but your soul and heart and innermost feelings too. He didn't do that to me yet. He didn't need to. I skipped over white gloss leaving toe prints and smudges and made tea for him. We sat together before the huge open fire in the sitting room where he told me my home was not my own. I remember he used the word *doormat.* He said, *These people walk all over you.* These people who I lived with, who had set up home and had children and built a life. Who had taken care of the farm while I went off to be smashed by a cult masquerading as a drama school. Who were happy. He said I'd lost control. This sense of invasion was hardly breaking news but the power of that moment was in its voicing, *your home is not your own.* I'd grown up in a house like that, a place overrun with guests my mother used to make up for the guilt of being rich. The commune was a beautiful attempt at another way of life and a replica of this stab at feeling better about wealth. And in naming it, he provided an answer; hey presto, it was him. He would sort it out, he would save me, all I had to do was close the commune and tell all the people to get out.

49

DOORMAT

A black fly buzzes about the kitchen as I write, small and annoying. It circles me, persistent and I'm not surprised. That was him, single-minded and obvious. Of all of them he was the worst, not because his delusion was any greater but for his intent. The others – the people who had crossed my path and abused their power – were convinced, if they thought about it at all, that they were doing me good as well as themselves. But he knew he wasn't. He was shooting fish in a barrel. That night by the fire, paint on my feet, I heard the word *doormat* and felt immediately frightened. I hadn't realised. He was right. I had to act. This is the way of the shattered brain. All it needs is a picture. He laid out in that hour drinking tea exactly what he would do, precisely how I would lose control at his hands by drawing a story of it already happened, a picture I walked right into. Not everyone on the commune was lovely but not one of them had gone out to cause me harm, they were people getting on with their lives in all their funny, normal ways. They trusted me. The first one I told was the woodsman, an original member who had kids at school, who was married to a Wiccan woman. They'd built a complex home in the bluebell copse, there were daffodils and paths, terraces edged with stone. We sat in the field, I said he and his family had a month to leave. His wife took a broom to my car, smashing it on all sides. A tall, skinny druid with the skew leather hat who'd lived quiet and happy played out his hurt in relentless speechless moments in the kitchen.. The road protester took his coffin and bag of oats. The old couple in the top wood left with shaking heads. I don't remember the megalithic giant going, but one day the metal barn was empty. I do remember finding hanging from a tree an effigy of me, a figure dangling by the neck within a triangle of sticks, a branch I would see on the path behind my house. The egg man kept out of the way. He'd played his first hand and gone back to London while I cleared the farm. The fucking coward. And when it was over, the commune dismantled, the people gone, the land empty of yurts and tipis and trucks and friends and drums and didgeridoos, he came back.

50

SHAMAN

It's going to be all right. This story that has been going from frying pan to fire has a happy outcome in the end. I feel the need to tell you that because from here on in it gets darker and the oh no what's next can be exhausting. So remember as we dive and the air becomes stifled and the pressure builds that there is a lowest point, and when we get there, we'll turn around and start coming up for air. We will survive. On his website he says he ran a clinic at the address of my farm; just a line in his bio that gives the lie of something simple and complete. To fury, upset, anger and outrage I cleared the farm while he waited in the safety of his north London flat. When everyone was gone, their lives uprooted, the commune dismantled, my car smashed, the effigy of me hanging by the neck broken into pieces and thrown onto the forest floor he returned and set up home in the bedroom down the hall. I thought he was my saviour. He was charismatic, he exploded with energy, he was sort of handsome, he played the trumpet when he wasn't cracking eggs and blowing smoke. He was certain. He had an answer for everything. Shamanism is flashy, impressive, a mystery to which he liked to hold the keys, a gatekeeper, master of the arts. It was exciting. It felt as if the old life was cleared away and something new begun; new people, new language, drumming replaced by jazz solos. No more pagan ceremonies, now the altars had South American iconography, Mayan symbols, the incense changed from sage to copal. Eggs were bought by the tray. Even as I write this, I can feel him listening. That's the strength of it, truth doesn't matter, if he really can hear me or not. He believed completely in his power and so did we, the support crew, the entourage, the floozies and flouncies, the set up that kept him in place and us looking only at him and not at each other. I have lived in these worlds between worlds and I know the rules and the no rules. Anything is possible. But I write this anyway because I know he cannot touch me. He is a fly buzzing in a jar. A boy from Kent who needed to feel better about himself. A magician who failed to read the small print. So we set up a clinic in the studio in the garden and the people came.

51

A BLANK WALL OF SILENCE

There's a blank wall of silence in my mind when I try and think back, to capture the essence of what it was like to live and work with a boy from Kent who called himself a shaman, who's still out there, working. I'm exhausted by it. I don't know where to start. Is it enough to say that we ran sweat lodges every three weeks, hordes of naked crying people crawling in and out of a pitch-dark dome in the mud while he intoned and chanted and spat water, hot rocks hissing? How we stood about afterwards, flushed and confused eating baked potatoes. The hauling of those heavy blankets onto strings in the barn to dry in time for the next one, how everyone wanted to feel like they were his special helper. How he skipped about the kitchen, a firecracker of energy, taking up all the space. How he let me be seduced by him – and I've worded that sentence carefully because I knew, even at the time, that he had no interest in me as a lover. Yet that was my language of devotion and he needed me to stay at heel so that's what he did; he let me in occasionally, just often enough for me to feel that between us there was something precious. If only women talked to each other. How much time we'd save if instead of staring up at some fucker we turned to each other and compared notes. Did I mention his long-suffering girlfriend? No, nor did he, not until he was properly ensconced, feet firmly under the table. And once we'd all got used to that reality he brought in his Spanish lover, she who he said was a shaman too, his equal, and no, I didn't take offence at the inference, I just lay in bed listening to them having sex down the hall. My god he rode roughshod, it's shocking to think of it now. And I believed in him. I believed every word he said. What he didn't say but should have, if he'd had an ounce of conscience, was that he wanted the farm, its beauty and power, the sheer force of these hills and land, he wanted it all to himself. And he got it, almost. That's the trouble with shamans, the White ones anyway, the ones not born of the lineage, they think we're all idiots. They think the power is in them. If he hadn't got high on his own supply and overplayed his hand, I'd have lost this place. But he did.

52

BUCKLE UP

He went to Mexico for the summer to see his teacher leaving me in charge of the sweat lodge altar. I cleaned and lit and waved incense and genuflected but the candles turned black. He said it was an attack, he was always in battle with dark forces. I wrote my first novel over those six weeks, a story of a girl who goes to India and loses her mind. When he returned, I put it in a drawer. We went to Italy to run a sweat lodge on the shores of a lake near Rome. We went to Wales to collect more basalt for the lodge at home. I went to Valencia for a month in an effort to keep up with his Spanish lover. His Spanish lover came to stay and he ran her about the garden in a wheelbarrow, she, screaming with delight. He made coffee and forgot to fill the base with water and the espresso pot exploded hurling burning Lavazza all over the ceiling and he laughed and thought it was funny and I grabbed cloths thinking, *This is my kitchen*. He said there was a black panther resting on a branch near the sweat lodge fire. He didn't identify the trouble in my bones. He had a tall, angular, male devoted helper on hand to do his bidding. He had legions of beautiful female patients; one had ankles causing her suffering, he assured her he could make them slim. These are the signs, not a candle turning black but devotees and lack of care and stupid promises, the keen use of the title Shaman. Because anyone who calls themselves that probably isn't. Because power without awareness is force, and force runs out. I was lying in the bath when he came in to talk to me. I don't remember what he said that made the first penny drop, but I remember thinking, *He's never going to love me,* and it was a revelatory bomb going off in my head. I knew I had to leave. Not him leave, mind. Me. I was still up to my neck in belief of him. The beautiful patient with the imperfect ankles invited me to Australia, she said there were parties, it would be fun. I bought a ticket, packed a bag, left the boy from Kent with his eggs and copal and lovers at the farm and boarded a flight to Sydney with the fat ankle girl who looked down at me from a willowy six-foot height. And while I'm on that flight, because it's long and there's time and the choices I made when I landed need context, I'm going to take you to the place all of this has been driving at. Buckle up. Put your seats in the upright position. We're going back in time, to 1974 and a tall, cold house in London.

53

LIKE KEYSER SÖZE,
WAS GONE

When I was three a man turned up to live in the basement flat with the woman who'd escaped the Czech revolution. She, a refugee, had been given a job and a home by my mother, he was her husband, not Czech, probably Australian or from New Zealand. It's likely she married him for Commonwealth residency, I've spoken to other Czech refugees who knew her and that is their best guess. Our home, the tall, cold house in London, was a place of many rooms and many lives; bohemian, socialist, crowded, wealthy, artistic, noisy and lonely and trying to track the details of one particular person is like chasing a ghost. My mother recalls him as handsome and freckled, blond hair. Someone else has compared him to Donny Osmond. Another is adamant she doesn't remember him. One person called him a *memory implant,* someone else said *shadowy,* there's a report of him cooking eggs in the kitchen, no one remembers speaking to him. I can find no details of who he was or where he came from and this haze speaks volumes of a person who was there for nearly three years and, like Keyser Söze, was gone. If it weren't for the fact that he'd remained for me a memory unbroken, his name and the truth of him would have sunk entirely. But I never forgot him. In my mind, unquestioned, he'd had the title *first love*, a mystery figure who'd paid me attention in a house where it was scarce. I had nothing to base this conviction on, it just sat there like a sticker on a box I carried around as I travelled through my life searching for what was wrong, no memories for illustration except this one, the day of his leaving. We were in the hall by the big black front door, I was nearly six. He crouched down before me and told me he had to go but he would take me with him. I was to pack a bag and wait for him in the garden. I ran upstairs, fetched my rainbow rucksack, goodness knows what I put in it but I put it on my back and went outside and sat on the wooden bridge that linked the playroom glass doors to the patch of grass and I waited. And I waited and when I couldn't wait any longer, I walked to the end of the street and then I walked home, in through the big black front door and this person who I'd been willing to leave with was gone and his existence never mentioned and it was as if he had never existed at all.

54

THREE OTHER MEMORIES

Here are three other memories I carried unbroken and unquestioned. Every night I would slide down the banister of the tall, cold house, curving polished wood beside stone, and when I reached the dark ground floor, I'd slide all the way up again. But one night I didn't. I waited, my legs dangling, waiting as I had outside for him, and realising slowly that with him the magic had gone. I remember dismounting, my pyjamas and bare feet, and having to walk the stairs instead, up and up in the pitch-quiet of a sleeping house knowing it was over, it would never happen again. Let's roll back a bit. She who had married that shadow man arrived when I was one; this photograph, the only one with her in it has only her white sandal, we were in the square garden opposite. My mother's socialist heart wouldn't let a bit of out of your depth in the way of doing good, thousands had fled oppression and my mother had opened her door. Which is admirable except trauma is not a state to put in charge of your children. She had curly red hair; she wore fuzzy peach jumpers. She was bad before he left but after she was worse.

I remember this. Bedtime. Crouching behind my door. Hearing her searching for me. She pulls me out of hiding. I am in jeans, not ready for bed, she is angry. The window is open. She drags me across the carpet, lifts me up and pushes me out onto the wide sill streaked with London grime. I feel the wind that blows through the branches of the trees in the square garden opposite. She is holding me by the waist. She is screaming that she will drop me. We are five floors up. I look down and see the black iron spikes of the railings. Afterwards, perhaps it was days or weeks, I am sitting on the big chest freezer in the basement while my mother, in tights and shirt, is ironing her skirt. She is in a hurry. She is going out. I am banging my Kicker shoes against the white wall. I tell her what happened. She puts down the iron, circles the board and hits me across the face. She tells me I am never to speak of a person like that. She says, *These poor people have nothing.* These potted memories are important for the story they told to my little mind, and the one which they tell to me now. They're going to make sense. There will be understanding. But look, wait, do you remember? We're on a flight to Australia. Look out the window. You will see the lights of Sydney. We are coming into land.

55

A PARTY OUT THE BACK
OF MULLUM

Do you remember? A party out the back of Mullum, a lake, an Australian night. I was high and you were wild or was it the other way round. I'd dumped my willowy friend with the ankles she was ashamed of soon after arriving in Sydney and jumped in with a bunch of Israelis who had a camper van going north. She was furious, she said she'd *offered me her friendship on a silver platter*, a phrase I found funny not sobering. It didn't make me sorry. The Israelis called me *hefty* or some such word which is relevant to mention not because I was but because I soon wouldn't be, and I hadn't noticed that through a cult and a shaman I had grown fat. I felt innocent against their world view. I tried to talk politics and they laughed. Their motto was dance don't speak. I had forgotten the Israeli from long ago who had made me mute. They took me to parties, that party, the one where I met you. By the time we reached it I was with one of them, he was small, he had curly hair. We were camped on the other side of the lake but I was bored of their talk already, their exclusive cool. I took mushrooms and went in search of something else. Perhaps I was looking for a cafe though there weren't any, but I found that awning and that ground and I lay beside you for hours enraptured by your profile in the dark while you gabbled I don't know what. Then music took us and we were gone, into the night, the dance floor, it was not until the next day that I saw you again, saw you properly for the first time, crouched barefoot on a speaker, your camera, dreadlocks, torn leggings, ragged vest, shark's hook earrings, those rings on your fingers and bangles up your arms, a terrifying handsome man. I went to the lake and knowing you were watching took off all my clothes and dived in. I lost you again and then I found you, I'd danced all day and went in search amongst the tents and vans for a ruby red VW with the back open. You leaned out and looked at me, tipped your glasses, revealed blue eyes and I knew, it was inevitable, we would have children though I still didn't know your name.

56

THE FIRST NEEDLE

We left the party and moved in together. It was that simple. There was a house which two beautiful Japanese boys had found; I had been staying there with the Israelis before I came to the party on the lake. I told you about it and we drove out, found a window open, climbed in. It was wooden floors in a jungle, brightly coloured rugs under eaves, dripping leaves in an Australian storm, tree frogs and kookaburras calling. It was clean and bright and beautiful and furnished and empty and we took it without asking, it appeared to be made all for us. Those three months we spent in that house in Possum Creek, they were the best of us, they were water unchartered without letting each other down and shouting. I peroxided my hair. You introduced me to your friends. We rolled through thunderstorms, picnicked on the floor, made a nest of art all our own. And early on you introduced me to something else, too. We were on a dirt road, a steep drop away to our left, the jungle rising to our right on our way to a party when you pulled over and told me to hold out my arm. Was it speed the first time? I think so.

I think it was after that we moved on to methamphetamine, once I had a taste for a taste which I had instantly. You gave me my first needle but you weren't to know how much I'd love it, how it met with the longing I'd had since forever and made a dance with it. Or were you? I've thought about this for a long time, this question of responsibility because you said hold out your arm and I did and it cannot be undone. I cannot un-know and maybe you didn't want to be alone in the knowing and after that dirt road you weren't. You had a partner in the secret about finding god and discovering him absent. We could be faithless together. Needles are for those who've been abandoned and need to prove it. They are the evidence for loneliness and neglect. I flexed my arm against the sting, felt the speed in my veins, you put the car into gear, we drove on.

57

INVINCIBLE

There is a version of this story where you stayed in the jungle, and I came back to England and our relationship remained three addictive magical months in a house in Possum Creek and none of the terrible happened and none of the beautiful either. But that isn't this version because when my visa ran out and I had to leave I returned to a boy from Kent who was still trying to take over my home – remember? The shaman is still there, still cracking eggs, some other poor mug hauling sweat lodge blankets from the dome to strings in the barn. And I was mad about you. And I hadn't had nearly enough. So when I returned to England I rang you and said, *Come,* and I sent you a ticket and you arrived like a bird of paradise into the grey, muted lines of Heathrow, emerging through arrivals with wings folded, hair piled, a being from another world you may as well have had arrows on your back for all the difference you were to the ordinariness of English luggage trolleys and coffee shop chairs and square, dusty air. I had a thirtieth birthday party. I introduced you to my friends. I had left them large and soft round the edges, brown hair, un-pierced and come back a peroxide stick, a wild man at my side, your shark's hook earring, tattoos and rings and I think they looked at each other and thought, *Okay,* and said, privately, *Jesus.* I remember all the things unsaid at the table like *Who is this guy* and *What's happened* and I remember not caring because we were in our bubble and we were staying there. We found cocaine to go in our needles instead of crystal meth which we had swapped to in Australia instead of speed because it made us invincible. It cannot be unknown; it cannot be undone. It sealed up, in those early days, all the fear and all the dread and cocaine did the same when we couldn't get hold of it in England. We locked ourselves away and built altars to our art and the shaman skipped from room to room not knowing what to make of it, of you who held him in no regard whatsoever. You had come from a land of unbroken lineage to holy powerful people, you didn't give the boy from Kent half a second of your time. You said, *Let's go to an eclipse party in Zambia,* and we went.

58

CRACK DADDY WANTED

That was the kind of party it was. A thousand people on a plot of land in Zambia, gathered for an eclipse. We'd flown to Jo'burg with hand luggage of toy guns because scaring the shit out of people at parties was what you were into. We'd hired a car, ripped out the seats and turned the back into a bed and driven from South Africa through Botswana to Livingstone. God knows how we found the site; these were the days before mobile phones and satnav, we probably had a piece of paper and a map. I don't remember much about the journey except for sitting on the edge of a mattress, red sheets, white walls, in some motel we'd stopped in trying to find things to stick in our arm – wine, day nurse, crushed-up paracetamol, anything to stem the flow of craving that without our usual supplies of cocaine and crystal meth was driving us mad. But we found the party and parked up at an intersection of paths under a tree and found the drugs other people had bought out with them and I remember one night very high in the darkness of the back of that car having a vision of you at the gates of hell because that's where I'd found you and that's where I tried to bring you back from. And when I wasn't in the back of that car I danced and danced, all of us entranced by the repetitive simplicity of beats, all night and all day, nothing stopping us but for the eclipse which happened suddenly to shouts and brought us all to a stop and me to my knees. A silence on a ridge, silhouettes lined up, three minutes of wonder as day became night became day. *Crack daddy wanted* – that was the sign around the neck of my friend who I met, who was beside me through the chaos that came after because the party didn't end there. A week on that site, dancing without stop and then a hundred of us went on to the after-party, the Zambezi River, the island.

59

THE ISLAND

I'm not sure what happened except we'd been up for a week under an eclipse and instead of going to bed about a hundred of us decided to carry on. The island was a narrow strip of land in the Zambezi River, the only way to it by canoe. We left our vehicles on the banks, I don't remember what gear we had, I'm pretty sure we didn't have a tent but someone must have lent us one because you spent a lot of time in it. There was a bar, and a dance floor picked out by lights and DJ, speakers marked the corners. There was a fire pit with chairs and stumps and a couple of long drops that a friend soon fell into while tripping and never really recovered. The other person who didn't recover was you. There was a routine. Take acid around sunset and dance through the night and into the next day and just when it felt like we were straight enough to make decisions take more acid so we couldn't. Day after day this ragged band growing more ragged, unable to leave the island. I had visions. It became desperate and impossible. And then something snapped in your head. The first thing I knew you'd written *cunt* in magic marker all over the bar and the men who ran the island wanted to kill you. You hid in your tent. Then word travelled that you'd be selling something you shouldn't and other people, not just the men who ran the island, wanted to kill you. So my crack daddy friend and I dragged you out at dusk into a canoe and across the Zambezi with crocodiles snapping and hippos snorting and into our red car. The moon was coming up, we bundled you in the back, my friend pinned you down, I took the wheel. The tracks were sand, interweaving, criss-crossing, no idea which way to go, at speed, frightened of getting bogged or lost or chased, stranded in the Zambian bush, men out to kill you, you struggling to escape, screaming at us from the well of the back seat. I took a wrong turn, a fallen tree blocked our path, if I'd stopped that would have been it, I put my foot down, the car jumped. We landed on the other side and sand flew beneath the wheels, a song played on the stereo, when I hear it now it takes me back exactly. And when we found ourselves at a tarmac road, the full moon in the wide African sky I got out of the car onto my knees and cried. I took us to a hotel. But then you broke your foot and got out your magic marker again while we were having breakfast.

60

THIN CRAZED WHITE GIRL

The same word, written over and over, all over the hotel bedroom wall. And he was gone. In another version of this story I apologised to the hotel staff, paid for the paintwork, got in my red car, drove to Jo'burg and flew home alone and none of the terrible happened and neither of the brilliant either. There was nothing to stop me. He'd likely be dead but what did I care. I'd tried. He and his toy guns and broken foot and magic marker could meet their fate and I'd be safely on a plane out of there. But that isn't what happened. We found him on the banks of the Zambezi trying to get a lift across to the island. He'd hitched there from the hotel. I don't know how we got him in the car. All I remember is leaving my friend in Livingstone and setting off for the border with him beside me, torn black leggings, bare foot up on the dash, and being stopped by the police. Their shocked faces when this thin, crazed White girl didn't behave with deference, screamed at them instead because that's what I do when I'm cornered, because by then I'd had enough and I'd lost all sense of sensible. How they threw our passports at me from the window of their car and drove away. All I could think about was reaching the airport when I would never have to see him again. I could throw his passport at him, get on that plane, be gone. We stayed in a glass-fronted hotel the night before the flight, he in another room, a bottle of whisky. He turned up at boarding. I remember how the air hostess came to me in distress, how they threatened to land the plane if he didn't stop raging and abusing and frightening the other passengers half to death. And that would have been it, the goal post moved again to reaching the UK; as soon as we were home, I was out of there, I was sending him away, this bird of paradise whose feathers had turned ragged, I was telling him for certain it was over. But I had forgotten the shaman who waited for us at the farm, his takeover ready, who'd had a month to shore up his plans, who'd cut the brakes on my car and locked the doors.

61

WHEN CRAZY MET CRAZY

It's now that the shaman overplays his hand. You'd think cutting the brakes on my car and locking me out of my house would have done it. Or throwing a party while I was away called *Going Ape* that he'd advertised with fliers all over the local town. Or his misogyny. Or megalomania but don't forget context; I'd come out of India, Israel, commune, cult, and Centro Maya was just another chapter in an already overloaded book. And he'd got inside my head because even the most poundshop shaman knows enough tricks to make it look like they know a lot. The bulbs are flashing again in the kitchen as I write this, that little boy from Kent, annoying as the bluebottle circling my head; I'd better get on with it. After I'd climbed in through the bathroom window and left the car nose-first in a fence I met the shaman in the kitchen. He said, *You have to take the stone circle down,* and that was when I knew. The realisation that he'd hit my edge, the boundary across which I would not go was sudden and disappointing. I remember thinking, *Oh. You're an idiot. This is the moment when crazy met crazy.* The bird of paradise appeared wearing a magician's hat, tall and felt and covered in stars, the rest of him naked but for my dressing gown which flapped open. He broke into the shaman's temple, stole a bow and arrow from the altar and snapped it over his knee. The shaman was incandescent. Rage made him drop all pretence. He took chase. They ran about the garden. The shaman called his henchmen. The bird locked himself in the car. The shaman sat exhausted and powerless on the stone steps and said my family and home would be cursed for a thousand years. The sink in the downstairs cloakroom spontaneously fell off the wall. The bird stayed in the car. I walked the shaman down the drive to the main road. I told him he was not welcome. I said he could never come back. The last I saw of him was on that road, standing alone, small and defeated. He wrote to me once, years later, a badly worded email with grammatical errors saying it was about time he thanked me for his time at the farm. Not actually thanking me mind, just saying he probably should. He's still out there, buzzing around. He can thank me now if the years since have brought him an ounce of the wisdom he lacked. Meanwhile the bird of paradise with the wings grown ragged got to stay in his stead, and with him the needles and parties.

62

WE DROVE THEM WILD

At the heart of addiction lies trauma. It's an answer to the question *How can I live with such pain*. My love affair with needles was a problem-solver and like all dysfunctional relationships it began with explosive belief that I'd found the one and ended with my world reduced to a pinprick. For three years I travelled back and forth to Australia using crystal meth and cocaine to make life feel better and for a while it worked. I was stick thin and unapproachable but to a degree I was happy. My friends and I partied in remote and beautiful places, liberated in trance for days at a time, pounding the earth, our bodies loose, all rules abandoned, an ironing board for a bar, an inflatable for a pool party, ketamine and vodka for breakfast, we drove them wild. I made friendships that I cherish to this day and I see how close I sailed to the edge and it takes my breath. It was magic and it was terrible and we're lucky to have had it and come out of it alive and some of us didn't. But temporarily it solved the problem, how can I live with such pain while not telling me what the pain was, a deal that by the third year was just me and my gear in a room and the most fleeting of escapes. Because addicts are chasing the feeling of finding the answer and it's never as good as the first time. By the third year I'd cut all connections, what did I need other people for, they just got in the way. I cannot pass a parked car in a lay-by without thinking the people inside have stopped for a taste and when I think of the ritual my cells remember. I have lain in the bath and apologised to my body and my veins have stood up in my arms and my blood has pulsed visibly and let me be clear, the body does hold the score, it is conscious, it forgives and it remembers everything. The end came at a party in Australia, not an outdoor trance delight but a room in a house where we'd gathered, the people there linked not by friendship but by method. I was lying in a bed; bodies were scattered about and on either side of me were two people with needles in their arms. I remember having a moment of seeing the scene as if new, without irrational explanations. I remember thinking, *what am I doing?* It was so sudden and so obvious. I got up and left, flew back to England, never used again. I felt I'd got off light until I understood it wasn't needles or crystal meth or cocaine that I was addicted to, but something deeper.

63

GREMLINS

I'm going to tell you a fairy story. Once upon a time there was a little girl who saw something. She happened upon a woman in a bath who was drinking a glass of wine and the woman's expression said she saw it too but she carried on drinking her wine. The little girl knew she was going to die so she took what was most precious inside her and gave it to the Gremlins who lived in the hollow of roots beneath the trees that grew on steep cliffs behind her father's house. And then the bad things happened to her, the things she had seen that would surely end her life, and a million pieces of her were split in a million ways, shattered and sent spinning and she put those pieces in a black box marked *my first love* and then she grew up. She forgot about the box. She forgot about the one precious piece of her she had saved and given to the Gremlins to keep safe. She forgot she had once been whole. Years went by. Voices in her head telling her she was shit made her run. She left home and picked up speed. She tried every which way to outpace them but no matter how quick or how nimble, the voices chased after, grew louder, and she didn't dare look behind her; she feared they'd grown into an army. If she stopped she would die so she blocked her ears and closed her eyes and ran faster. But one day, tired and exhausted by the fight to not see and not hear, she stopped. The Gremlin wobbled up to her, delivering its message. Not an army but a single round and hairy beast from her childhood who had lived in the hollow of roots behind her father's house. She thought it was going to tell her how bad she was, how worthless and useless but instead, as it grew closer, she heard a different voice, and the voice said, *Help.* The Gremlin stood quiet as she reached inside it and there, trapped but alive, was the one precious part of her that she had forgotten. She held it to her chest. She felt it click into place. The Gremlin wobbled away and the million pieces of her that had been shattered and sent spinning came spinning back.

64

A MATTER OF SURVIVAL

Bad things happened in the basement of that house. It's taken a long time for me to say that. The pictures of my childhood never made sense, why I was so frightened and unhappy, why I built an armour and ran away and kept running. We had such plenty, enormous wealth, a revolving door of parties, artists, cocktails in the drawing room, these spoilt children, our mother would say, don't you know how lucky you are. Yet at its heart was something dark that left us splintered. The woman who escaped the Czech revolution who was given the job of being our nanny was troubled, but her husband, the shadow who lasted three years was worse. He faded into myth, the truth shut up in a black box marked *my first love* while she took the role as star tormentor, the one we could blame, her psychotic presence, the horror of her in our lives was not forgotten. She was ill and my mother didn't have the heart to cope. When she screamed about the house, convinced we plotted methods of her torture, my mother would say, *Cruel children, these people have nothing.* And when she banged the pipes in the basement my mother would crouch beside me and say, *We can't leave the house in case she burns it down,* and we would cancel plans to go out. She was arrested eventually, for running the streets in her underwear, I heard she was taken to a nunnery. And I left home and started my own race to outpace the demons in my head, answering the question *how can I live with such pain* by building an armoured heart and taking a lot of drugs; a search to make it my fault was an answer in itself. I married for a second time, had children, my father died, I got divorced, throughout it all, from childhood to changing nappies, I wrote. I published a novel about someone else's pain; my father, his mother, and it gave me liberation of sorts but still I didn't know. The pictures of my childhood, these fragments I'd remembered, sliding up the bannisters at night, the day the shadow man promised to take me with him, weren't enough to create a whole, until one day it happened. I was sitting at my kitchen table researching author websites, flicking through images when I came upon a woman in a bath holding a glass of wine. It was not like the actual I had seen as a child but it didn't matter to that lock and key in my head. Something clicked and the black box opened and those pictures I had hidden as a matter of survival came tumbling out onto the floor and I saw.

65

RECOVERY IS FOR
ANOTHER BOOK

It's funny to think that within days of the black box opening I headed off to the Venice Biennale, that most surreal and picturesque of places which on a normal day is like walking into a dream, but which during the festival is beyond Alice in Wonderland. The missing pieces of the jigsaw had come tumbling out, I had a seen a picture awful but whole, ugly but a thousand times better than the jumbled nonsense I had lived with; memories that made no sense, feelings that had no grounding, behaviour at odds with a childhood apparently so blessed, and the revelation was like taking acid as my world changed shape and settled into its new reality. It was with this that I landed in Italy and pulled my suitcase noisy along the cobbled canals, Venice out of body, an explosion of art for which I had no grip. I spent three days lonely and drinking and out of my mind, putting on a show for the people I knew so that they would not know, spinning with all the shattered pieces of me around this one fantastical, unavoidable truth. Now I knew, and the pictures came together, and I had to live conscious with what had been hidden. Recovery is for another book; it is an ongoing process but I will say this. Within a year of remembering I stopped drinking. I'd been a steady wine-in-the-afternoon-on-my-own sort of person, combined with spliffs it had been for over a decade my way of connecting with the thing that was lost. Abuse splits you off from yourself and I was seeking that person, all addicts are doing the same, at the heart of all addiction lies trauma. But those couple of hours every day manufacturing a feeling of not being alone cut me off from twenty-three other hours of connecting properly, and it was time, so I stopped. I cried for a month. Then the sensation of acid again as if I was tripping. By the third month sober I'd found my feet. It's saved my life. I have saved my life. When I started this memoir, I didn't know the sun around which it would orbit, the story I was telling. That only became clear as I wrote, that most magic of knowings, the unconscious, driving the story of a girl running blind, acting out, being lost until she is found. I found her in a gremlin, in a black box, in words on the page and this thirty-thousand-foot view of my life has been a gift; I have seen patterns, a way through, the picture, again, has made sense. I don't know how to end a memoir. I suppose you do it like this.

The Recovery Diaries

I AM ALWAYS HAPPY
TO SEE YOU

What did happen next? Okay, I'll tell you. The black box opened, the missing pieces fell out all over the floor, my world turned upside down, I went to Venice and then I came back, and the work began. I went to my therapist and said the words I'd never said, and I doubted myself completely. She asked me if I'd ever made anything else up, if I'd ever before willingly and knowingly deceived someone into believing a story that wasn't true. I said no. She said there are certain unwavering flags of the survivor, and doubting your own story is one of them. I said I had a metallic taste in my mouth and my head felt like it was in a clamp. She said the body cannot lie and the metallic taste is shock. She told me to read Waking The Tiger. I was still drinking and smoking, I hadn't realised that part where stillness is required, I was still lighting fires and washing them out. I don't remember who I told. My ManPerson, definitely. A friend in America who rang when I was sitting in my car having just done an interview on live TV because in my literary working life in that first summer of knowing I was also promoting my debut; realising a dream for which I'd worked so hard it made me cry like I cried when

I told this friend in America, the adrenaline rushing and the surreal simultaneous truth spilling out in the car park of Sky TV. In that first summer, this new reality that was terrible yet I was better for it would often come to me while I was being someone else. More often than not I would shake my head and say no, I must have made it up, it was a moment of madness, an attention-seeking spat. I'd try to reassemble the old picture; a childhood of glamour and basic neglect in a tall, cold house in London, a busy, absent mother, a loving, absent father, wayward, unfathomable people tasked with our care. Yet the body cannot lie and it would revolt and say, *No. Look. See how that picture frightens you while the other calms you down.* And it was true. The other with its horror made everything settle. The overwhelming feeling of seeing it was relief. The body cannot lie. When autumn came, I embarked on a self-prescribed course of medical marijuana, illegal but quietly done and designed to begin the healing of my battered nervous system; six months of careful dose. I carried on smoking and drinking. It was 2019, you can guess what's coming, news was filtering out of a virus, a friend who'd been in Wuhan came home and was terribly ill. Christmas came and went. My therapist recommended I see a colleague trained in Somatic Experiencing. I made an appointment. In four years' time I'd recognise the state of emotional flashback I'm in almost a hundred percent of the time, and learn to say to that child, *I am always happy to see you,* but back then everything was new. I was identified. I hadn't met the parts that rise up in their varying attempts to protect her. With the Somatic Experiencing therapist I would. I would learn to not push her away. I am always happy to see you.

MOHAWK

I'm going to tell you a story. Another one. They said, having explained exactly what was involved, "Volunteers?" One hand shot up. Eyebrows were raised. Notes on clipboards were checked. They said, "Are you sure?" As usual it was a matter of overestimating ability while underestimating the task. "Yes, sure." I don't even think you looked up. You definitely hadn't been concentrating. "And you've understood the finer points." "Oh, totally." Thoughts wandering onto something else. "You'll forget completely." Yawn. "And you'll believe totally that you're alone." *Yeah, yeah.* "And you won't remember us at all." "Got it." But you didn't believe that was possible. A tube, a hurtle downward, a red haze, a place contained within a pulse, another tube, the access to your breathing, this place, *this place* and you had forgotten, and you believed totally that you were alone and you had to breathe through *that* – as if you must put your mouth to a tunnel of faeces and suck. *I have to depend on this?* Already I knew it would kill me, the toxic gas of it, the unresolved, unprocessed shame that was my only source of life. I remember the recoil, but or else you would die and so you put yourself to it. You breathed in. When I think of that girl who wasn't anything yet, a bunch of cells that had formed around a spirit, or rather a fleshy vehicle into which you hurtled all gung-ho and *what problem?* the devastation of that moment, the complete forgetting, I know it started there. I got a Mohawk this week, my hair cut into a middle-aged White woman warrior and a friend asked me, Wh*at's the significance?* Everything I do is survival. Every move a rescue. I am saying, *Look at me now. I am unafraid.* I am being unafraid for you, while you are afraid all the time.

AFTER PANDORA

A long time ago when I was still in the throes of crystal meth, I wrote a novel called *After Pandora*. As a crystal meth baby, it was a crazy melange of over a hundred characters, each with a point of view. It was unprintable but there was something to it – it was talking about parts. I look back at that unreadable novel and know I was trying to say something. These are the parts I've met: there was a teenager trapped in a room with a high-up window and no doors. There was a sprite trapped inside a gremlin. There was a ten-year-old sociopath sitting on the basement steps. There was a girl, frozen, five years old, staring at a wall. There was a baby, horrified at the womb and her birth. There was a griffin, tail slapping, blue blood dripping from its click-clack beak. There was an angel, sixty foot high, so large I could only see its feet. There was a woman made all over of green. I've met them at stages of recovery, witnessed some in action, seen others change. In the room of the teenager, I discovered there was a door. We opened it. A chair appeared in which my therapist sat and read the paper, patient. The teenager climbed down from the windowsill and, over time, left the room. The fairy sprite that was trapped inside the gremlin we already know was delivered in the form of basic gremlin words that I misheard for years and ran from, believing it was chasing me to tell me I was shit. When at last I took Pema Chödrön's advice, stopped, turned around, invited the demon in, had tea in its mouth, it wobbled up to me in its hairy, butterball way, short legs and skewed teeth and I heard the voice saying, *Help.* That fairy sprite was released from its place which had begun as its safekeeping. I fixed her back inside me with a click. The ten-year-old sociopath, we'll call her Rosie, who sat on the stairs, her eyes on the basement flat door, I had believed was waiting for the shadow-man out of love and desire. But when I sat with her, I realised that was wrong. She wasn't waiting for him to come out or come home so as to be with him, she was on guard. If she had eyes on his whereabouts, she could protect. With some persuasion we got her into the hall where the wall of small square panes of glass allowed her to look through for a while, still keep her eyes on the movements in the basement. And then she allowed us to move her away, to believe, as we gently said over many weeks, that the danger was passed, her job was done, she could stand down. The sixty-foot angel carried her out, gathered in its enormous arms. It sat her on a cloud. That Angel took up the baby too and held her. Is still holding her wrapped tight into its chest. The woman made of green appeared again and again, her healing hands. And one night I had a dream that I was walking through a house I knew and, as happens in dreams, came upon a whole separate other bit that wasn't there in waking. This other bit was the colour of absence; a beige, tan nothingness, not so much empty as neglected. Sparse furniture, the feel of an interior nobody cared about much, no effort had been made to make it look nice, it had the basics but no more. I walked through it and arrived at a space down three steps that was in almost complete darkness except I could see on its other side a huge ornate door. I stopped on the brink of that room and woke up. In meditation and therapy I returned to that brink again and again and gradually it changed. First the fairy sprite turned up at a table at its centre, I could see her lit by a candle that blew in the breeze of an open window behind her. At the table she writes and writes and the pages fly up and fly out of the window and she is happy and determined and whenever she looks up, she makes a face and sometimes she lies on the chaise longue behind her and comfortably smokes, one arm crooked behind her head, her legs outstretched and her ankles crossed, and thinks of what she is writing. With more light I could see the ornate door more clearly. It was open sometimes and beyond it was a road. But mostly it was shut or just a bit ajar and the griffin sits in front of it and its tail slaps the steps and it raises its head and barks its click-clack sound and blue blood drips from its beak. The sixty-foot Angel is there, so large I can only see its feet. I know it holds the baby, less horrified now, comforted, recovering from its nightmare of shock, asleep. On the brink leading down into the room, a wide descent of three steps, sat Rosie, her back to me, the woman of green had her arm around her. I have watched her bleed and knives fall, I have seen her wrapped in green and held and known she took my place in that basement. She suffered so I wouldn't have to. The Green Woman held her for weeks and weeks, I returned every day to the scene and for ages the scene didn't change. The Sprite at the table, writing by candlelight, the pages flying out of the window. The sixty-foot Angel, its feet so large, in its arms held to its chest, the baby. The Griffin slapping its tale and lifting its beak click-clack keeping guard at the ornate door which was ajar. Rosie bleeding knives as the Green Woman held her. And then one day she was back on her feet, she was standing legs wide, feet planted, her messy jeans and T-shirt, one hand on her hip, the other pointing at me, she was saying, *You.* She had red eyes. I have watched her leave that sunken room and trace her way back through the house to the place where the five-year-old stands frozen, facing a wall. I have seen her grab that five-year-old and hold her, her body ever the shield. She is sociopathic in her determination to protect. She knows only that, this five-year-old and her mission. Don't put Rosie in charge of relationships. I have learnt that. She cares about nothing and no one but the five-year-old child and the charge of her protection. She holds her, her body a shield, the five-year-old frozen.

A DEATH ON REPEAT

I've been thinking about death and rescue, how much of what I do is motivated by them. Let me explain: if I'm a famous novelist I'll be saved. If I don't grow fat or old or ugly, rescue will arrive. If I meet every deadline, complete every task, make no mistake ever, death will be averted. All of which implies I think I need saving. That frozen five-year-old is suspended in the moment of knowledge before the event. She knows she's going to die and as she has no one to turn to, she thinks the responsibility of saving herself lies with her. Also, the blame if she fails which she will again and again not because she is useless or fat or old or ugly or talentless or scared or lazy or unpleasant or annoying but because she is five and her death is inevitable. Here's another point. The reason why the famous novelist bit works is because it will make me big enough to be noticed and implicitly say I must be pretty special, leading, inexorably, to my rescue. That's the subtext: the reason no one's coming is because they don't know I exist. So, this is what I said to her as I ran through the woods one morning: the reason they're not coming is not because they don't know. It's because they don't care. And the reason they don't care is not because you're not worthy but because they are preoccupied with their own suffering. They know you exist, but that doesn't change a thing. It doesn't matter how big or famous you get they still won't realise they're failing you. No amount of success or shouting is going to make them aware. You can stand down. Also, it isn't your fault that they don't realise. It's their problem, not yours. It's not a comment on your worth or a reflection of your value. It's a comment on their parenting. Which is quite shit. And then I said this: go ahead and die. Accept the worst is happening. Instead of fighting the horror of what's coming, surrender to it. Let go. You're not alone. I'm with you. I can't die for you but I can stand by you, accompany you to the door and I will be there on the other side to greet you. So let yourself die. Then the whole rescue thing can be dropped. I won't have to be a famous novelist or put every waking minute into the losing battle with age. Fat and ugly will no longer be weapons in your hands, I can be imperfect. We can all relax. So, she died. I watched her through scenarios; falling five flights onto metal railings, a death in the basement, being disappeared the day of the rainbow rucksack. Over and over, we played out her death as I ran through the woods, feet pounding, breath loud; she fell, was torn apart, vanished. We saw her funeral, the lives after, the regret and grief, the mourning. We watched it all. A death on repeat in that house so that I can stop holding my breath, frozen in that moment, waiting for it to come.

A MARCH ON MY SENSES

It's been a rough few days. Not Putin rough, though actually now you mention it – an ally turned critic, a critic turned rogue and a march on Moscow, maybe not so dissimilar after all. It started, when? At pushback of dissent? At misuse of power? At the moment it was given mouth and eyes, the switch flicked? Home-made monsters will be monstrous at home in the end. It's their M.O. Mine's been telling me everybody hates me, I'm a failure, my life's work a loss. These exacting, effective bullets and bombs. I armed it. For weeks I obsessed that I'd upset someone I care about, to the point where I considered my life at an end, only to see them by chance and it be normal and the utter darkness of cornered thinking to lift like the shroud it was. I had a brief spell in the sunshine, the relief of living again, only to wake up one morning in the catacombs. Was it because I'd been pushing back? I've been reading *Complex PTSD* by Pete Walker and putting it into action. It's not a laugh a minute but it is effective. I've been telling the ally turned critic, the critic turned rogue to fuck off. Who are you to tell me I'm worthless? Fuck you. But then the beating began. The fear. The intimidation. The march on my senses. I woke in a blackened world. I told myself I was on strike, I couldn't do it anymore, I work and work and work and I get nowhere. This *work* flipped between my exterior literary life and my interior recovery. I spoke to my ManPerson on the proviso he didn't give any patsys. No trite *this will pass* or reasonable argument to the contrary. My son threw a packet of goji berries at the counter and hit the cactus I've been nurturing, breaking a limb, snapping babies. I lost my shit. Said, *Can you just go away for a minute?* and went away myself and cried. I hunkered down, waiting for slaughter. I snapped at a friend on the phone who suggested what worked for him. I said I didn't want to talk about it. And then an ally brokered a deal, an unsure peace, a march on my senses arrested by going to London and celebrating the success of someone else, a book launch that I know has taken all the blood and sweat and tears that this writer friend could cope with. My home-made monster has gone off to Belarus. And when I said there'd be no repercussions, I was lying.

EAT THE RICH

I'm going to tackle my father. Not literally, physical was not his language, and also, he's dead, so that's not going to work. But I mean here. In these pages. Because everybody hates the rich, right? So now I have to talk about it. Here goes. He was very wealthy. Money was a language he did understand. Also, he was charming, good company, a laugh when he was in the mood. Not ha-ha jokes funny, but outrageous funny. He'd say, *I fucked a girl in that telephone box,* as we drove past it and make me gasp at the outlandishness and be tingled by the intimacy. Any information he gave, even inappropriate morsels of his private life, were grabbed up and treasured. He sailed his own boat, he rarely let anyone aboard and when he did, could throw them off at a moment's notice without explanation or apology. He was reserved and enticing, a captain I stared at. His great grandfather was a Duke. His mother grew up in a castle. His great uncle married a Princess. People jumped to attention when he was in the room. Everybody wanted a piece of him. He was handsome and clever and mercurial. He kept to himself and winning his love was an essential childhood mission. He was sold by his mother to his aunt for £500, a fact he shared casually.

I wrote about it in *A Perfect Explanation*. So yes, I get it. His was a world of wealth and neglect, monetary riches and emotional poverty. A privileged man in twentieth-century Britain, a child of empire. I became rich because of him, and to a child in a tall, cold house in London, he was king. But he didn't live with us. Early on in their strange un-togetherness my parents settled on a system where he mostly lived on his large West Sussex estate, while we lived mostly on his London one. At weekends we gathered in the country, an explosion of children into a chocolate box cottage on a Friday night that had him disappearing to his studio. He was a writer, he published biographies of eccentric Victorians. He could have lived in a castle, too but chose a low-beamed cottage on the side of a road, so picturesque and pretty that tourists stopped to photograph us while we were having lunch. Weekends were the big opportunity to win his love which I did by cutting his tomatoes just right for his salad, presenting his margarine decanted and perfectly smoothed in a tiny white dish, trying not to get in the way, or be five or six or whatever age I was that was annoying and loud and messy. You knew you were in the good books when he invited you up to his studio to see the gallery, a private museum of treasures accessed through a secret door that held wonders like a pair of Queen Victoria's gloves. Even there, there was a test. Could you slide the keys down the banister rail so that they dropped into the Wellington boot at the bottom? Only sometimes. He was a man of games and trinkets, he wore slippers with bells on, you could set your watch by his ordered life. Occasionally he came to London. The housekeeper would whip into a frenzy, my mother's waifs and strays shooed out of the kitchen with a dishcloth, the kettle boiled. There'd be a different air in the house as he crouched unhappily at the end of the table, bow tie and three-piece suit, cradling his tea or sipping his Cinzano. One of disappointment and annoyance. He carried a lemon in his pocket in case my mother didn't have any. He required ice to be ready for his drink. He kept his hands smooth with E45. Have I given impression enough of someone unassailable? He held the power and here's the point I'm trying to get to. In all the years of therapeutic work, the untangling of what happened, I've only ever held my mother to account. But mothers are easy to blame, aren't they? They are there and they fall short. I used to say he wasn't, so how could he know. But here's the truth. Even now, fifteen years after his death, if I say one word like *failed,* all hell breaks loose in my mind, the sky crashes in, disaster reigns and rains. I let him off the hook because I loved him. Because he was a man. Because he loved me, and he made me rich and in case from beyond the grave he takes that last vestige of protection away.

I WANT TO TALK ABOUT
JEALOUSY, I WANT TO TALK
ABOUT PRAISE

I want to talk about jealousy. I want to talk about praise. Those are the two lines I wrote this week, one after the other, as prompts to a post I was yet to figure out. In my Complex PTSD brain, praise is transactional. If it's given, I must work to keep it. If I'm not grateful enough, it'll be withdrawn. It's precarious, not a gift out of nowhere from a stranger or a friend, no strings attached but something intimate that intimates threat, a cold wind about to blow, a high pedestal from which I can be knocked. I think, *Shit, now I've got to work to keep it* and *That person hates me* or is about to. It's immediately weaponised. It becomes a matter of isolation and I react to it like risk turned up a notch. I'm jealous of other lives. Mick Jagger makes me depressed; Helena Bonham Carter makes me lonely, and Giffords Circus makes me certain I've taken a wrong turn. I compare my insides to their outsides as if they have no trouble or pain. I objectify them and dehumanise. My outside looks like my photograph and my inside looks like a Francis Bacon painting. My outside is relatively organised, and I can list easily my achievements and pieces of luck, the aspects that make up what people know of me and see. My inside looks like a Francis Bacon painting. The truth is that my life was stolen, to the extent that abuse is theft. The experience causes the survivor to imagine there's another path going on into the distance without them, another life, the one they were supposed to have. That sensation gets translated into false pictures. I watch a Rolling Stones documentary and think, *There it is, the life I was supposed to have!* and I get depressed. And the same when I meet Helena Bonham Carter at a party or hear about Giffords Circus, I think, *I may as well give up now.* I'm not a musician by the way. Or an actor or an acrobat. I've never aspired to any of those lives. I don't know why they get it in the neck and not Margaret Atwood. It must be the sheer fame that they represent, the stellar height, their imagined untouchable-ness. They must in some way represent safety for me. It was the grooming that got me into it in the first place, the position where something precious could be stolen. And that's how these paths converge, where these two ideas meet, these lines, these lives that rattled around my brain this week – I want to talk about jealousy, I want to talk about praise. There's the connecting tissue. The outsides of people I don't know, the insides of misdirection, the idea that anything can be got wrong, praise as threat. I'm avoiding ending this on something pithy about destiny, about how there's no other life but this one, how all experiences make us but I'm not convinced I'm succeeding.

THOUGHTS ON
THE EUROSTAR

Tearing through France on the Eurostar I think I've hit an impasse with writing – I'm waiting for notes on a novel from my agent, I'm lining up to pitch the memoir, I've got the third book in a series bouncing on its toes and stretching its calves on the sidelines, just out of sight, on the periphery of my vision. So what now while I wait and stretch? I've written about the events that made me, I've written about my mother (have I? Now I think of it, maybe I haven't), I've written about my father (yes, tick, definitely done that) and I've written a bit about recovery (have I talked about sobriety? Cold baths? Somatic Experiencing? No, not yet). And so as I write this, I see places I can go apart from the south of France towards which I am barrelling on the Eurostar with my sons and ManPerson (who hates that phrase but I hate boyfriend, partner, all those others, too young-sounding, too cold-sounding). There are options, any one of those I can pick but more than anything is picking the blank page, and seeing what pours out. Like this. Unedited and unguarded. Good for me. And also the immediacy which is what made the memoir so effective (for me – its effect on me) because it was every day, it was have to, it was press publish no matter what. So stand by people (and already I want to apologise for the imposition, the emails that will come barrelling into your inboxes) for a new tempo, or a revert to the old tempo, of daily. It's good for me to be unguarded, to not edit to within an inch of my life, to find a way round the carefully curated presentation of thoughts. It drives home the truth that nobody cares in the way I think they do and everybody cares in the way I think they don't.

LUCK

I'm in my happy place, literally the place I feel happiest, a house in the south of France that my father bought in the late sixties, and that by luck and chance now belongs to me. It sits on a crystal mountain on the edge of a national park, it's a complicated series of hallways and stairs, rooms leading off rooms, roofs intersecting, the result of an ancient farmhouse being augmented over the years to become she, madam, this villa we refer to as the monastery where shadows cannot hide. She is alive. Over the years guests have come here and seen bits about themselves, about each other. In the long hot afternoons tempers have frayed and come together. It's a revealing place where we cannot pretend for long anything about ourselves. I arrived last night tired from the slog of England, GCSEs, my own work, I woke this morning in a mood. It feels as if the snapping, growling frustrations of the year come pouring out and I wrestle with how lucky I am to be snapping and growling in such a place as this, but this is what it's for. This thing about being lucky and not having the right to complain is a dog-eared book my mother read to me like a riot act throughout my childhood. I know, of course I know, where she was coming from, but it didn't help.

It made me further than I ever was from the shared baseline of human emotions. I spoke to her yesterday and she said, *You're so lucky to be there,* and she meant it in a different way this time; lucky to be able to travel, to up and go while she is confined to her cottage in the countryside; bed to Zimmer to stairlift to wheelchair – this place that she loved too is now completely out of reach. But still she doesn't complain when she should, when she's every right as a human being to say, *Fuck I'm frustrated, tired, had enough.* When we would welcome any other answer than *fine* said not cheerily but with all the Don't Touch Me's of a person used to their armour. I wish sometimes she would cry. But she won't and I will. And then I'll up and be washed of the emotions I brought with me, that I carried from a year-long slog of England since the last summer I was here. This place is my respite. I am lucky. I think I want to write about her more. I shall pick her as my subject tomorrow. I will get stuck in.

GUILT

That was her thing. How she made me feel guilty. But maybe I don't put it all on her, my mother, maybe guilt was my response and she was off on some other trip, oblivious. But it's a state of craving I reach for easily, guilt that in some way I haven't come up to scratch in what's expected of me in a relationship – not the romantic intimate kind, I never feel guilt with ManPerson – the female friendship kind, that's where it gets deposed. From where it belongs to where it is easier to feel, somewhere not so close to the bone where I can gnaw on it. It was what the relationship with my mother was built on, little notes shoved under her bedroom door, *I'm sorry,* feeling as if all the troubles in the world were hers and all the fault, mine. It's how you build a narcissist. Funnily though, not ha-ha funny, but strangely I feel no guilt for her now, no direct sense of her discomfort and unhappy ending and my still grasp and grip on life, that she is stuck and I am free; I don't visit her much, I could visit much, much more and I feel no guilt about that whatsoever. I am hardened. I feel, *Good, I owe you nothing* which is harsh and harsh to admit. *I owe you nothing.* I've written her obituary in my head a thousand times, at least begun it, at least thought, *What will*

I say. Here in France in the house that she loved she was lilac Liberty shirts and thirty lengths of the pool, her handprint on the stones to count so she didn't have to, swimming fast to finish before the sun disappeared her mark. She was tomatoes gathered in a basket from the garden, and white sandals, and her feet that were so rarely up, up sometimes on the terrace, a book, old copies of The Architect's Journal that she'd packed in the Citroën along with us. Her obituary would say that she was a feminist icon outside the home and a patriarchal mother within, our brothers favoured, us girls told to stand up for ourselves. She taught me no was not an answer by telling me I didn't have it in me to succeed. With her I developed *fuck you.* Which is hard to say because now I know she is proud of my work and won't remember saying anything, but *I knew you had it in you.* Lilac Liberty shirts and tomatoes from the garden; I see the ghost of her here even though she is still alive in England. Guilt: I feel it snake into female relationships and I lay it at her door.

RELATIONSHIPS

Relationships, right? So difficult, so complicated, so necessary to growth. Note I don't say happiness there – I nearly did, my hand hovered and then the full stop hit instead. I'm not sure they're necessary for my happiness, and I'm talking romantic relationships here, the classic two-person bond of sex and intimacy. Friendships, absolutely vital but I was on my own for seven years and by the end, not knowing it was the end, I was happy. I remember thinking, if this is it, then that's okay. It's not like I haven't been round the block a thousand times, it's not like I haven't tried everything, and I was good, not looking, not searching at all and then wham, an old friend out of nowhere and a lunch and a truth I'd had no idea of. Let me back-pedal a little, an old friend – and to be clear, this is my ManPerson but at the time just an old friend, with whom I'd started exchanging email letters over a winter six years ago, my favourite thing, to have my brain tickled. I found myself looking for the reply, reading it quickly and taking my time to answer so that the pleasure of ball-in-my-court would be prolonged. I found myself having *feelings* – god forbid, and it was shocking. But still, just friends until the lunch when he told me he'd loved me for seventeen years, expecting nothing, actually expecting me to rebuff and say, *Yeah, all right that's sweet but anyway,* and his shock, almost appalled when I didn't, when I said, *Actually I've got feelings for you too.* Six years of the kind of ride you wouldn't send your kids on. Tempestuous, fraught, how we fought to stay together and failed many times and many times got back on the ride, always this golden thread between us, making us not ready to give in. And then recently a calm we have won, a different set of challenges, the steady, wide stream of a river in flow. We are utterly different, I have to stretch myself to meet his needs even halfway, and he likewise and that's where the growth comes in because I have become kinder, nicer, more fun and he has become braver, stronger, more disciplined. We've shared our qualities with each other. But still, relationships, right? Two adults with opposing inner-childs, a need for attention, a need to be left alone, a constant flux, we are in it for the growth. We always agree on that.

FIRE

The summer of the fire a praying mantis sat on a pineapple in the kitchen for so long that the fruit rotted beneath it. She was such a presence we didn't dare move her and she hardly moved herself, occasionally a shift to another frond, perhaps a turn around. I was told later, when I was recounting how our summer had played out oblivious to what was coming, that such a visit is a portent of protection in the face of danger. All hot July we paced about her, not eating pineapple, aware of her. And the earth cracked and the sun sizzled and rivers already dry dried further underground and a smoker made their way to a pit stop on the side of the motorway an hour by winding road away from us, ready to throw a cigarette out of a window, or not grind it out on the ground or not notice one tiny ember flying away into six hundred hectares of national forest which dipped and swayed in the push of hot wind. Was she still there when we packed our bags and left, thinking another glorious summer over, see you next year? I can't remember. But I remember waking at four in the morning to my phone buzzing, a message from the friends to whom I'd lent the house after we were gone, saying, *There's a fire, we've been evacuated, we've shut the shutters.* I sat up in bed, turned the light on, found a live map of the area burning, tried to figure out where in that vast smear of red was home. The horror of realising it was in the centre. And here's the extraordinary thing, because I'm sitting here now in that house, so yes, we know it survived but get this: the fire, the six hundred burning hectors of it, came right to the door. It burned the hammocks hanging between beams, it took out the tree beside my bedroom. It obliterated the lemon grove that edges the kitchen courtyard. Paintwork bubbled, a chair on the terrace melted. Everything in every direction was blackened to a swirling hot crisp, a garden wiped out, a forest gone. But it didn't touch the house, not even an inch of it. The ancient cypresses which stand as sentries at its corner remained completely unscathed. The pompiers stood in the pool, their hoses aimed at the wooden roof yet that cannot account for the miracle of it. We were engulfed. And a friend who lives nearby messaged me as I watched on my phone from England, after it was over and I had been up all night. She said, *It was as if an angel put its wings around it, I felt it, I could feel its presence.* A praying mantis came and told us to be ready. An angel came and put its wings around it. And when I told the taxi driver this story as we weaved through the scars of fire still apparent, winding up to the house this summer, she nodded and said yes as if this was normal.

SOBRIETY

I'm feeling sick today, and dizzy and a bit bitey. Friends are leaving, a changeover of guests and I can tell by my mood that it gets to me in subtle ways only identifiable since I've been sober. These emotional flashbacks – because that's what this is – used to form the fabric of my every day, the wallpaper of my world, I didn't know there was a house behind it, I thought what I felt was the truth about the present, not the past. What I'm getting to is this. Friends are leaving and the disturbance of it twangs those spider's web lines to the part of me still alive with the injury of leaving this magic place and returning to a tall, cold house in London. A friend also sober, also in recovery and a survivor says sobriety is like putting out fires, one by one, only then the work begins, the bit when I can see clearly enough what lies beneath the impulses that make me grumpy here or snappy there. Everything, and I mean everything, leads back to those formative years, from the womb until the armour was set, and that includes the intergenerational too because trauma only stays as trauma when the burying continues. It's hard, sobriety, sometimes, the sometimes when I want to get away from myself, or when I remember the myth of drinking, that first sip, the joining in of it. But on the way here the taxi driver said, *Oh yes, you're near St Maur*, a vineyard we love, the wine which we'd drink, it too was part of the fabric of my life here. And I said, *Yes, but I don't drink anymore,* and, in that moment, I remembered how I can't because it isn't one glass, it is a craving set off that is unstoppable. I was a very reasonable drinker, you'd never have known from the outside that I lived for that moment every afternoon when I would settle down with half a bottle and three spliffs and my laptop, a blank page or a story I was working on, that it was the highlight of my day. But I began to notice how only in those magic hours did I feel whole. And I noticed that the wholeness of me and a bottle and spliffs said a lot more about the rest of my life than I was comfortable with. When I stopped drinking, I cried for a month, and then the world went psychedelic and then time slowed down. Those are the things; an upsurge of feeling, a gauze removed, an experience of things becoming quieter.

AGEING

It's happening. I mean it's always been happening obviously, but you know what I mean. It's happening in obvious ways, by which I mean ways that I don't like. When does growing up cease to be called that? When I literally stopped heading upwards? Can't be because that happened back in my pre-twenties. Emotionally? I think we can all see from these posts that that's still very much in progress, although I will say I'm mostly an adult these days, able to tell when the child is having a tantrum or upset, less identified and more able to turn up for her. But at some point at which we all agree but can't collectively pin-point, it being such an internal dialogue and movable feast, so subjective it makes my head hurt, growing up becomes growing old. I am growing old. My jowls have made an appearance. I have iron grey shoots in my hair. My bingo wings are a source of amusement to my children. My eyes are going. My body can no longer tolerate high doses of sugar, or for that matter, anything. I must be temperate and steady and get my highs some other way. I am on a voyage inward, having voyaged outward to my full. But what does it look like, this ageing game that I'm lucky to be playing, the alternative being to be dead? There's harking back to photos of when I was young and realising how good I looked and how I didn't realise it at the time. There's the absolute certainty that I will look back at photos of myself now and think the exact same thing. There's the wild annoyance at twenty-year-olds publicising their anti-aging fit-for-life diets and exercise regimes. I shout at their animated faces on my screen that the reason they look like that is not because of kale and yoga, it's because they're twenty. They don't know about this stuff. They're not there yet. But they will be. And I try hard to not make that sound like a weapon, and vengeance, which it is sometimes when I feel cross and misunderstood. Because when I was young I'd look at people like me and think they'd let themselves go, if only they'd make an effort, it was sad. And for sure they think the same of me. Yet I know the truth of this ageing game too; its wildly unfair and brilliantly fair rules, the hand that I justify again and again, the story of erasing the story of shame that I would grow old at all.

SEX

Let's talk about sex, baby. I woke up with that in my head, not sex on my mind but that song on a loop, *Let's talk about sex, baby, let's talk about you and me.* Sex. Yup. It was the absolute centre of my world, the sun around which every decision revolved for most of my life including the early years when I didn't know that's what it was called, this thing that ruled me. Those urges were set off in me too young, this involvement in that fire; it was from the start a thing to be weaponised and traded. It was a power that consumed me. I remember being caught masturbating when I was a small child, the housekeeper walked in on me in the playroom, I was watching TV, lying on a huge pillow, the comfort of it followed by the shame. I know investigation is normal but it wasn't that, already it was a secret and a bond. I loved him, the abuser, and I could give him what he wanted. That's the bit, the modal of sex as a thing to be used. Not something beautiful to be picked up and put down at will but a trade-off and a fuel, the engine that sent me from one place to another, searching for the sense of completeness he gave me, the attention of him, the sense that in that space I existed. Writing the memoir was the first time I saw the pattern of this. It was double shocking to think I hadn't seen it at the time or until now. The thirty-thousand-foot view of my actions afforded me the revelation that years of therapy hadn't. I saw how events connected. And here I am at fifty-two, a lot of work done, much digging deep, much turning up, and hand in hand with that the menopause has happened and my relationship to sex has changed shape. What is it when it's not a commodity? When it's not dangerous? It exists now in a place spacious, unrefined, without consequence. It's no longer hard-edged. I don't use it to hate anymore. This tender, funny, heightened expression of connection, this playground it's taken me all my life to reach, perhaps that's normal too, the time needed to understand the sheer volume of it, the essence and magnitude. As I write this I feel sick, a familiar feeling of reaching into that place where the damage happened. It's so hard to associate this feeling with the actual because of course that's not how I remember it; that's how disassociation works, it literally takes you out of sensation. This is another aspect of the work, to stay present when intimacy happens. What a long road this is. I feel like I have to start again every day.

BEAUTY

I want to write about beauty – or rather I don't want to write about it at all but it keeps running around my head so I have to. It's annoying as I fear I'll be judged for it, and I fear it'll invite all the *but you are* and *it's within* that come with the subject which however sweet and lovely and sometimes thoroughly welcome are not where I'm going with this today. I want to strip it bare and talk about it objectively and say bald statements like *I was* and not invite the contrary. That all right with everyone, just this once? Okay. Here goes.

I was beautiful, I had my time, a classic beauty that makes men turn their heads and older women feel bad about themselves. Yesterday as we drove to dinner a girl reversed out of her house in a convertible mini and she had that, those lips, her sunglasses, an insouciance so casual it makes the hours spent in front of the mirror seem pathetic in the face of it. She turned her head to see us and stopped and we passed her and everyone in our car went wow, okay, there she is, and on we went. In town it was hot, I wore a long dress, the breeze wasn't enough, we walked up narrow, cobbled streets, ivy-draped houses, their shutters open, we were too early for our table. And there she was again, appearing out of an alley as we took a turn about the town to waste time, shorts and white vest, a cat in a carrier in her arms and she was looking again, I thought for the vet but it turned out for the restaurant next to the one we were aiming at. Taking her cat out to dinner with her friend, she sat with her back to us, smooth brown shoulder blades, blonde hair caught up in a twist, legs that didn't dimple on her chair. And so we talked about beauty as we ordered tagine and the burnt pink flowers draped through ivy around us. My sons, after some coaxing, named a person at school they thought beautiful, coaxing because we had to get past the *it's subjective* phase and be clear I was asking about conventional beauty without judgement on better or worse. My ManPerson named easily the girl who'd been It when he was young. Then the question, why did we all name women, and so we thought of men, too, famous ones, trying to sum up the essence. We found it hard to talk about without making it personal, what does it imply about us as if it's a prize earned rather than a passing phase that means nothing. It opens so many doors, it invites so much comment, it's something everyone is encouraged to want. Then I was asked, *Who was it at your school, don't say it was you,* but it was, beauty like the girl with the cat. I was aware of it. It got so much attention. I was taught it mattered. And then it was gone, and yes that other beauty, the one we all possess took over that's so much harder to value yet which means so much more, that isn't a passing phase, that is deep and universal and without compare. See, even I who is in charge of this page cannot stop myself from ending on that note, *inner beauty, kindness, wisdom, we are all so much more beautiful now.*

VISIONS

When I was a child I saw a pair of brown trousers walking down the stairs. There are many reasons why no one believed me, mainly the ridiculousness of it, but then again, that's its strong point. Why would I make that up? A ghost floating would be easier, more standard, but it wasn't a ghost. It was a pair of brown trousers. I was about five or six years old – I can't be certain because most of my memories I pin to that era and they can't all have happened then but five turning six was a coming of age for me, when the shadow man left and after that I appear to have blanked until I was eleven. So let's say I was six, my birthday come and gone the Easter before in this French house, I remember that for the card in the shape of the number that I hung on my bedroom door where it turned upside down on the handle, a six become nine, and felt immeasurably sad, my knees up, my back against the headboard of my bed. But this was summer, we were back in France, and I'd been out by the pool when I heard the telephone ring, a landline, this was the seventies, its trill reached through glass doors, across gravel and uneven stones over which I raced to the cool of the terracotta, eager to answer because what? It was exciting, useful, who knows. It stopped as I got there, the silence after noise a noise in itself, a ring ringing in my head but nowhere else and the hall felt bigger, quieter, on the edge of something as if my hurtle from water to house had hurtled me across dimensions and into a looking glass world. The rocking chair began to rock. A pair of brown trousers walked down the stairs. And when they vanished I returned to the pool with what I'd seen tucked under my arm, a vision unquestioned, I accepted it. I'm recounting this because we've just moved the furniture in the bedroom that used to be mine, that had a doorway to the hall which was bricked up and a new one cut so that the bathroom is now opposite but it changed the energy of the place and my son, who's sleeping in there and hates that room couldn't sleep. We can't undo the bricking up but we've moved the looming wardrobe with the secret drawers and shifted the beds so that they're not cut in half by a beam. And I said, I can put a sentry at the outside door if you like, this other exit that's always been there that leads to the garden, and I imagined the being that I'd seen when I was five who reappeared the summer of the fire, who we all saw this time in brown hat and jacket, the same brown, a colour I recognised who appeared to everyone that year until we realised and shared and some of us were spooked but I wasn't because I knew. The room is rearranged, the sentry is at the outside door, the beams no longer cut the bed, the wardrobe with the secret drawers no longer looms and six-year-old me is an echo through a door bricked up of a birthday card hung upside down on the door handle to the hall, don't come in.

CRAVING

I have a craving, I can feel it, it's like a demon snake dragon with spiked tail whipping, fangs and eyes, the scales of it. I've had it since I arrived here in France, this house that sits on a crystal mountain brings out the truth in everyone including me who is made of its walls, who is encased in it. I've wanted to smoke and drink, connect is what it is, I remember this feeling from the old days when I did just that, take myself off with a bottle and spliff and blank screen to divulge and indulge and be completely whole in consumption. This urge, this driving to connect. When I began Somatic Experiencing, in the very first session, the place I came was here, the swimming pool where underwater I saw a being drawn by William Blake in its sinews, the exactitude of its muscles, the way they were long and thin and binding. This creature with arms and legs longer than human, thinner, more muscular, was crouched in suspension of water, turning slowly with weightlessness, its knees up to its ribcage, held by see-through arms, holding itself to itself and it was red, like rusted iron, like old blood. A pain body made real to my eyes, I knew it as that as I saw it and swam next to it, watched it unfurl and swim away, a something made of me, come out of me. I've been seeing it again, the memory of it when I swim in the actual pool, not projected when eyes closed I'm in the hands of the therapist but in real time here. I see it, the memory of it each time I go underwater. Have I talked about Somatic Experiencing? Not really, I mean to, it's so delicate, so personal of course. That creature that was pain filtered, that had become full, that swam away contained the blood, it was a function of my being, is a function for these emotions and sensations which can kill you in the end. I imagined a new filter like changing one under the sink, and the process begins again. The Somatic Experiencing – that is lifting trauma from the body, that is letting the body speak directly to the therapist – it has taken me to familiarity with the multiple worlds within worlds. These things existing all the time, my coffee, this desk, on holiday, a craving, holding all of it at once, or at least moving through it without causing a breakage, is an art I must talk about, try to talk about here. I try and sit still and notice.

SISTERS

You know that house of many rooms, many familiar, easy, happy to welcome people in, let them look around and then the passageway dark and a hand on the door stopped, no, not that one, you can't go in there? Those are the rooms I want to open up. There is one that I'm standing outside today and it makes me sick to think of turning the handle. It's marked sisters. I have three but there is one who dominates. I am the youngest of all of them but there is one who appeared master to me. Even this, which will not throw her to the lions, which is about my perception, feels betraying, as if she will rise up and curse me though she never did that, she always said she was looking out for me. I was her doll, I trailed after her, she loves me deeply, she held the keys to our father. She was glamourous, beautiful, blonde, popular, funny. I was dependent on her for reading the room, knowing what to say, how to act, do it right. Upsetting her was the worst thing ever, to fall out of favour I would scramble over hot coals to get it back again. She was my world. I looked to her for everything. And then one day I wrote a book about our father, his upbringing, the fight between his mother and her sister and when it came to publishing it my sister said, *Don't do it.* I know why. I understand but it was the first time in our relationship when I held something in my hands more precious than her. And so I published it and she and I didn't speak for a very long time. It broke something that needed breaking. It was a drawing of breath after decades of holding it. I didn't die. From this distance I've a clearer view of what all that was about, not the fight over the book but the dynamic of our relationship that was. And this post which began in my head about insecurities – that's what I thought I was going to write about today – it led from an easy sunny room where everyone is welcome down a dark passageway, a hand reaching out to a door, the sight made my throat catch. Because my insecurities, which appear fifteen times a day as certainty I've upset someone, were born and nurtured in that room. The spider's web line twanged, the vibration tickling the air in the shuttered space where she sits, the fear that I have lost her favour, that I am lost without her. I remind myself twenty times a day as I trace the line that she was a child, too. She was a child.

THE MONASTERY

Today we go to the monastery, an annual pilgrimage my mother made with us when we were small and it was a ruin, and one I make now with my friends. One of my sons is coming, the other wants to stay home. There are high winds today, doors banging and leaves flying, it will be cooler, the drive is an hour up and up the winding road, a sheer and terrifying drop to one side, the other steep rising mountains. I will go slowly. I will irritate the cars behind me. There will be cyclists sweating their way in pretend Tour de France, there will be madmen on motorbikes. We will park and walk the last kilometre of sandy track; the monastery will appear through the trees as it has for hundreds of years.

Except it was closed due to the high winds and fire risk, a ban on visitors who won't be as careful as the nuns and caretakers, who might have a swift cigarette in the car park and set off a blaze. We hadn't gone straight there, instead detouring to Collobrièrs far beneath it where in the past we've retreated for lunch following a visit. The narrow road twists to the valley where a wide river sunk between high walls is dry but verdant. There are cafés on bridges and the one we stopped at in the Place de Marie, a view of French flags strung across shaded square. As we walked in circles looking for the post office, a cashpoint, money needed, we passed a man at another little café, a single table outside, two chairs, he was in one of them, an ankle on a knee. He was on the phone and something in the slant of him reminded me of hot days in Australia, dropping down from our jungle house into the local town for supplies, two junkies on a day out that was really only an hour or two before retreating to our lair. Those days of obsession when all we thought about was getting it right, the next taste, did we have everything, could we hole up for the days needed. I remember how we'd search for houses out of the way where we could be left alone, like the monastery, remote and difficult to reach. I remember a landlady in a wide Queenslander realising what we were up to in her basement flat and throwing us out, how we got more wizened and scurrilous and secretive as the months and years went by. It consumed us, the totality of it, the way it filled our world; there was nothing but needles and the drugs we put in them. We built altars. We felt like aliens. We did not encourage visitors either. Now I pass me by in a hot market square, that small world encased in foot up, ankle on knee, on the phone, a coffee and cigarette before getting back to the business of a singular point. A tenderness we guarded like the gardens of the monastery. A devotion that would end.

NOTHING TO SAY

My mind is a blank today. I've come upstairs to write and I've got nothing. I've started and stopped five times. It's funny when that happens, and it doesn't happen often, but this task I've set myself, to post something every day, lays me bare to it. So here we are and I shall describe the room. I'm at what was my father's desk, now mine. An ancient, cracked leather inlaid into wood, a miniature balustrade of brassy iron criss-crossed around three sides, his lamp a sixties swell of brown, his book prop a cockerel of heavy black iron framed square, two strings with weights attached that would have held the pages open. The drawers have secret drawers within, the scent of him will still drift up when I open them, even though it's been sixteen years since his death. I've hardly touched what's inside, you know how it is with love and grief, we preserve, we can't help ourselves, it's as if perhaps one day he'll need that stapler. Opposite is the single bed he sometimes used when he didn't want to sleep with my mother, a dressing room bed, like a suitcase packed, on reserve and ever ready. It sits against a wall of huge, floor-to-ceiling painted scene, a man with an axe raised to a tree that is barely alive, just branches at the top, the rest bends in extended brown trunk, how has it not yet fallen over. A dog watches him, it sits next to a basket. In the background a stone house, an open door and women and as the wall curves to the left the scene curves with it to a Punch and Judy box on crossed stilts and a child watching. To the right of the tree about to be axed is a river, a bridge, a man with a wheelbarrow, another fishing. I've been with this scene so much that my eye accepts every part of it. This, now I look at it all and remember, is my favourite bedroom of all time, partly for that painted wall and this desk, partly because it is split level, and at the steps, stone and the width of the room, a sliding door of pure sixties chequered orange concertinas it in half, or rather a third, to this privacy and cool that my father would have loved before me. It could be 1969, the year he bought this house; from where I sit there's not a sign of anything more modern except this laptop, the fact that I am tip-tapping away while he would have used a pen and paper; I don't think he worked out here, his word processor or typewriter, I don't remember him using them but he wrote letters. The headed paper is still in the drawers too, and his pens. I'm going to take a photograph so that you can see what I see. I'm going to post this for the practice of writing something when I have nothing to say.

A TICKLING

It calls to me, this thing I'm doing, I was lying by the pool when I heard it tickle. It waits for me to sit down, open my laptop, be here. I rarely know what I'm going to write. Today in the morning sunshine that slants from the back casting shadows of bougainvillea across our sun beds, not yet the laser heat of afternoon when we'll move the parasols to find shade, we talked about psychedelics in medicine and the use of ketamine. It's the only one that's already legal in the UK, a clinic in Bristol is rolling out its use for PTSD, anxiety, chronic pain and depression. We used to use it a lot in Australia, not the we who drink our coffee together here but me and old friends from there who brought it from India disguised as rose water. We used to dry it out on plates in that harsh light, the crystals appearing in sparkling form on tin. Mostly we snorted it at parties, a breakfast of champions, a line and a shot of vodka at the ironing board we used as a bar, but my friend liked to mainline and I did it a few times to see. I was telling my friend here how I never knew the depth and breadth of its psychedelic properties until I shot it in my veins and it shot me, faster than DMT, a supersonic speed to the place of its existence, so fast I recall a travel sickness, a

A Party In A Hurricane

Too Fucking Serene

Image copyright Sara Leigh Lewis
www.saraleighlewis.co.uk

Like A Third Eye In A Skull

A Day Out With My Father

Let's Build A Stone Circle By Hand

How We Learnt To Move Rocks

The Wedding

Like Keyzer Söze Was Gone

We Drove Them Wild

Little Paints

Image copyright Sarah Nunan
saranunan-illustration.co.uk

Service Games

Birthday Parties

Queen Of The Gypsies

(image copyright Tate Images)

G-force too much. She loved it. I stepped back. It frightened me. And now its medicinal use is at the forefront of medicine, this way to help people who've tried everything else; I hope it will become the first port of call, not the last, and I don't mean ketamine singularly but all of them, the march of psychedelics as medicine. I've been practising a DIY version for quite a while now. Six months before the black box opened in my head and all the truths came tumbling out, the jigsaw puzzle made sensible and complete, I'd been taking high-grade THC in capsules, not knowing but feeling the call and the drive, that tickling, the same that brings me every day to here, to say something out loud. A wider knowing, a drop of consciousness that knows itself as part of a whole, that has the whole picture. On my best days this experience of that connection is all the connection I need.

A DAY AT THE BEACH

A day at the beach, we come home hot and sandy, never drink enough water, the wind keeping us cool, the waves crashing, the noise of it. Once upon a time this beach had hardly anyone on it, a jewel we knew of, a restaurant run by a renegade, he flew a pirate's flag and told you off if you didn't finish your salad or ordered too many frites. He was handsome and suave and French and wild, his wife we mistook for his mother a thousand times over until someone made the faux-pas and was corrected, but he didn't stop loving us, unlike others to whom he would refuse entry. He served moules and plates of warm goat's cheese, we drank wine and lolled in the shade amongst cactuses, my children were small and burnt and wore baseball caps and sat for hours on the rocks. And then one summer he was gone, and his restaurant of simplicity, wood and bamboo unpainted replaced by a terrible light blue nothing like the sea or sky, and music, music! The first time we heard it we were shocked that anyone could think the sea needed it. And waiters in uniform, prices doubled, where was our pirate? We were told the story by the guy who owned the photography shop where we'd go at the end of each summer to collect the beautiful black and white portraits taken at the beach of our children growing, great groups of them posed that hang on the walls of the stairs and hall in England that the children dismissed as stupid and annoying at the time but now that they understand how time passes, they love them and show their friends. The guy in the photography shop said that they, the council had always hated Luc for his nonplaying by the rules, for the anarchic way of him. They'd searched for an error in his paperwork, a small mistake and found one. He hadn't ticked some box or marked some line, the smallest of absences in an officious hunt and it was enough. He was booted from his outcrop, the sea crashing in his wake, the pirate flag torn down, the moules gone, the cactuses thrown into the rough scrub beyond. His prize taken – was it him who'd paid for such scrutiny? – but his prize taken by the playboy from Brittany who'd always fancied himself a beach restaurateur. Our place has become an Ibiza lookalike, the prices doubled, the mattresses closer together, the clientele brash and shouting over colourful cocktails. We still love it. We still go. I'm still greeted by name though it's not the same. No amount of money can buy an atmosphere or cast a magic spell. A year after he lost his throne a massive heart attack knocked him to the ground, a heart broken by a stupid Brittany playboy who probably wouldn't notice, wouldn't care, who saw something and craved for it and shouted for it until it was his. He will never be Luc. He has the look of a man always discontent. And the sea still crashes and we come home covered in sand.

SIXTEEN YEARS AGO
YESTERDAY

My father died sixteen years ago yesterday. You might think I'd have written about him yesterday, I did too, but I didn't. I was taken over with the beach, he didn't cross my mind at the moment of sitting with the blank page which is probably a good sign. I don't mourn him now how I have before, a strike which took, having newborn twins at the time, three years to surface. But even then, even in the early years of this anniversary, I wasn't struck down with grief but more with a memory of that day, how strange it was. I was woken by my babies crying, they were three months old, I hadn't slept more than a few hours in a row since they were born, I must have been demented. I remember sitting on a mattress on the floor with one of them in my arms and looking at my phone and seeing a missed call or a message, I don't recall which, but whatever it was it made me haul arse; two babies crying for milk, a change bag grabbed, my husband at the time probably helped pack the car in a hurry, we were a forty-five-minute drive away. We'd known my father was dying, his was the most graceful of exits, a sudden blow-up of the body and within a month he was gone, none of the indignity of my mother. The many pills and medications had got on top of each other, his system decided it was enough and shut down. In hospital where he went briefly, they called the Macmillan nurses, he sent them out and gave away his cygnet ring when I was in the room to my brother, the most touching of moments to vie with others which made me rage and be forced to remember that this was his death, he could do it any way he pleased. When I turned up too early, before he'd had his shave, I was sent out too despite two little boys and breastfeeding and the hour drive and the impossibility of getting it right. Then it was home to the cottage on the quiet country lane, where he was sent to die, and the trouping of old friends, a queue that stretched to America. I waited in the kitchen. Endless smiles and tea and hugs, we all wanted our perfect ending. When it came time for my little bit of him I weighed up the possibility of being snapped at as his last words to me versus a happy loving memory of chatting days ago when I'd got my visit right. I chose to drive away, not say goodbye, quite certain it would be the last and it was. On the day of his death we raced those country lanes, babies in the back and ran out of petrol a few miles short, had to stop, took the time it took for him to die to fill up the car and get going again. Those ten minutes too late, my brother outside shaking his head. I sat with his body. My mother and one of my sisters said, *Where has he gone?* as if I would know. And I saw beings sweeping some distant floor above us, time and space bent to make them miniature, and a door shut behind them. And his body was empty and I didn't mourn what was not there. But driving home that night, two babies sleeping, the petrol tank full but my forgiveness empty, I thought how can the sun set on this day, it is rude, uncaring, it cannot be.

ONE DAY IT WILL STOP

I'm lethargic today. Hot. The south of France close about me. We got up early from a late night to meet with a new gardener to whom I pointed at tiny green sprouts emerging through gravel and walls and said, *I love them. These are my friends.* If he thought I was an eccentric roast beef he didn't show it. So lucky to have land to care for, I wade relentlessly against the tide of neat, explaining again and again to the teams who work for me that I don't believe in weeds. When I took on this garden it was a plague of topiary and bare ground, roses that didn't belong here, watering systems costing the earth, hours of clipping costing more. And leaf-blowers. Christ. Save me from those. We're changing teams from one who nodded and said yes and then filled up their machines with diesel and blew leaves anyway, uselessly from one pile to another as if the wind didn't exist, to this new man who is third generation of a family business, who suggested a watering hole for the forest animals. He understood our priority is fire and nature, to guard against one and nurture the other, that traditional aesthetics come nowhere. I used the word *sauvage*. This place is thirty hectares of land, a steep forest and some lower fields, one of which I'm returning to forest, the other rented to a local farmer for grapes. There are streams that we will clear, wells that we looked down as I did when I was small with my father, lifting the lid to find snakes and frogs, them and I terrified. There are reservoirs galore and an overflowing sceptic tank we call Lady Godiva though I don't remember why. There's the petite garden close to the house where roses were planted unnecessarily, and the lower, wilder bamboo and pine groves through which there once were paths until the fire destroyed everything, but we're going to cut them again. As children, to defy our mother's poor attempt to not let us drown while lunch was on, evaded the rope she strung across the gravel from olive tree to wall by skipping down into the thicket and emerging at the pool, certain we couldn't be seen. The steps have all been burnt but we shall put them back. We'll create it again for the children that will come here, let them think they are on an adventure and home in time for supper. And the trees too close to the house we'll remove and the giant ancient cypresses which guard two corners we'll leave, and we'll let the ground be covered by whichever survivors make the first move and the bushes will make their own shapes. In England I've done this, let it be wild, made the nurture of insects my priority and some people come and take a great breath and others say are you sure you don't want to power-wash the terrace or spray the nettles or pull out the thistles which blow great clouds across the fields. This habit of interference. Humans getting in the way, thinking they know best. One day it will stop.

LITTLE PAINTS

He called them *little paints* when he suggested they go for a walk together. This man who was my friend's friend but is no more for many reasons, one of them being a build-up of twatship and fuckery that buckled a human connection. *You can bring your little paints* to my friend who is mighty and exquisite, an artist in her bones and blood, the finest hand and eye but all he could focus on was the woman part of her seen through his own narrow view. We laugh about it now, we say to her, *Are you bringing your little paints?* when we go somewhere together, and we call him *#LittlePaints* – a joy in his foolishness that has long outlived his efforts at two people going for a walk. I get it too, not necessarily from men, but from anyone who watches this action of writing or imagines it and doesn't see the huge and difficult task behind it. *I've always rather thought of writing a book,* they'll say having asked me thirty seconds' worth of questions. *Well, go on then,* I think back, nodding, smiling, giving them the space to find out. But for all the annoyance we get the prize, don't we, us artists, we get to live the sheer wonder of it, sitting down before blank space, the magic. This direct line between me and god, and mine is a web not Christian man but the word is universal, you all know what I mean so I use it. This direct line between here and somewhere other than here, that it comes to me, to us, it's a wonder. Nowhere do I feel more complete, more whole than when I write, this contact that knows me absolutely. I feel words, the rhythm of sentences, I read them aloud and the tempo is obvious. They back up and pour out and have certain things to say, even sometimes, often, images and structures and uses of themselves that make no sense to me. Or rather they do but only as a whole, as if, if I tore them about into reasonable definitions, they would become gobbledygook yet together they work and I know that the thing that is trying to make itself known has succeeded. Writing, the transcription of sensation to language and onto the page is all about focus on these exacting points, like the man who focused his mind on the version of my friend he wanted to see. He told a story. Never mind that it was funny and exhausting, his was an act like this, a translation into words that spoke the tale of his world in one sentence. I almost love him for it if he wasn't such a park bench idiot for whom I have no time and neither does my friend who at this moment has gone off to paint. And I sit here and write and ideas say, *Explain me,* and I dig into these moments and can't resist and can't rest until I've got it right. These, my little paints. My little words.

THE GOD IN ME

Where is it, that line that divides the things I can talk about in public from the things I can't? Who sets it? Does it exist outside of me? Recently I was told off, quite gently mind, but told off for crossing it, a written line in a Substack breached somebody's moral boundary and they told me, too. Of course I'm not going to say what or who it was, that would breach my own, but I am going to talk about shutting down something uncomfortable and the instances where having to choose who suffers becomes an imperative. My reply was this – *there are times in this process when getting something off my chest becomes more important than protecting the privacy of others.* This didn't go down enormously well, but better than expected. A precedent was set quite a long time ago and it probably came as no surprise that I pushed back. This tap on the wrist was fair enough in terms of their right to say whatever the hell they wanted but it still got under my skin. I've always battled this, not in the sense of right speech, but in terms of upholding conspiracies and myths. I can't stand it. It makes me rage. Nothing causes me to abandon my values and kick the walls down quicker than being told to get back in my box. Aside from salacious

confidence breaking, or the incitement of violence or hatred
I'm okay with the risk of upsetting people. Artists having
been saying it for thousands of years but to hell with it, I'm
going to say it again: causing a disturbance is what art is
all about. Tip the goddamn apple cart. Throw the contents
everywhere. Let the rotten ones be strewn about. They'll only
infect the others. And yet I don't. I am so careful. I think of
the Melrose novels and faint at the amount of mess Edward
St Aubyn must have left rolling about the place. There are
so many stories I don't tell, so many people I resist from
mentioning by name, I have protected *so much*. And this
kind of thing makes me want to fling the doors open. They
said, *At least don't say these things in public,* and I replied,
But that's the point. The effort and risk and bareness of this
is what moves stuff and moving stuff is what this is all about.
I've avoided the cheap ticket of gratuitous beans a thousand
times over. Boy, the deletes, the multitudes of *okay, too far*
I've said to myself because the line – and to answer my own
question, it's inside me – the line is set exactly where growth
meets indulgence. I know it intimately. I trace its contours
every day. But the snarling artist in me says, *Fuck you all,* and
the responsible adult says, *I hear you,* and the little girl cries,
Don't leave me, and the shameless teenager has her finger on
the files deleted and the god in me says, *Wait.*

A MONASTERY IN TIBET

In the kitchen the pans clang like gongs in the wind where they hang, as if this were a monastery high up in Tibet, and I've been thinking about death. I said to my ManPerson, *Remember this will be the last thing you feel before you die,* as we talked on the subject of trauma. I meant his body, the sensations of it, that which is with us all the time until the plug is pulled, and as I said it two things struck me. Firstly that I quite fancied a high five for profundity, and secondly that I'd never thought the thought before. The conversation swept on, I didn't get the chance to dwell on either, so let's go back to it here. This will be the last thing I feel before I die, the sensations of this body I inhabit. Not only its sore back from playing tennis and foggy head from afternoon snooze but also the sensations of love and craving, loss and hunger, the actual things I feel now, translated into then but still the same. A whole heap of feelings then nothing. It's that bit that makes me stop and dig, that to be alive is to be tingling all the time, that I am made of nerve endings and these constant pings will be the last messages I receive. I have, instead of almost no information, almost all of it, everything but the leap, the what happens when the lights go off here and come on somewhere else. It brings death nearer, this thought, closer, as if up till now I'd imagined it like one does a holiday; perfect, just one person missing. But this is how death will feel, exactly like now only older. The desk pressing into the back of my forearms. The cushion pressing into my legs. My glasses indenting my nose, my bare feet on tiled floor. My jaw nudging its way to tense, a slight headache elbowing in. A loss and swell in my chest for my son who's going away. An ambition and gnawing for a novel that's with my agent, a worry that I won't achieve what means so much to me. A regret that I shouted when my children were young and just children and I should have known better. A love so big and enormous for this life it can cloud me and crowd me out. And then I'll be gone. And the pans will clang in the kitchen where they hang in the breeze like a monastery in Tibet.

THE BAYEUX TAPESTRY

Behind my bed is a panel of indented wall in which hangs a gift shop extract of the Bayeux Tapestry. It's been there for as long as I can remember, for as long as I've been alive. Likely my mother picked it up from the actual gift shop during one of her long detours from England to the south of France and hung it there when they first moved to this house, at the beginning of the 1970s. Last night a friend who's staying here woke up from a dream of walking with her beloved dog who died earlier this year. Disorientated, she went down to the kitchen and heard children's voices. She was half asleep and registered but didn't question, it was only when she got back into bed that she thought, *Hang on.* There have been high winds here lately and all of us search for the door that keeps banging but none of us can find it. I'm getting to how these are connected. Bear with. A while ago, asleep in England, I dreamt of this house as I often do, and in the dream I too was walking through the kitchen. Leaning around the island deep in chat were a whole host of characters, some in trilby hats, I remember thinking they were Spanish. I was conscious that they could see me, a ghost-like figure, pale and see-through, but that they weren't the least bit interested. What's more it was clear to me that this house was theirs, a feeling of home as deep and wide and certain as mine. I'm getting to the connection now. One night whilst actually here, I dreamt that the entire panel on which the gift shop Bayeux Tapestry hangs opened in a kind of sliding 1970s spaceship fashion and behind it was a whole other world. I saw mountains and fields and colours that are not here. And from that place my father's coffin slid into the room. The point is this. This place that we recognise as our house, the walls and floor of it, I imagine is a version of what else is here. I'm sure, convinced, quite certain that the people I saw leaning on the kitchen island talking, who could see me and were uninterested, are living here too, a dimension with more sides, they inhabit this space over and above us, our presence as normal as the wind. The dream that she was with her dog, my friend, the children's voices she heard, the Bayeux Tapestry hiding a panel that slides and hides another world, the door that bangs but none of us can find it, I said to my friend, *That's the entrance*. These people who watch me type, who move through me as I move through them, this tracing paper plane. I love the thought of this.

THIS ROOM

My son is working at my desk today, a lesson on zoom and so I've come to the sitting room to write, this space of many doors and pitched wooden ceiling. The terrace onto which it leads is an echo of this room outside, the same roof and dimensions, both stretch the whole length of the side of the house, both are split level. In here there's a free-standing fireplace at one end which divides the sitting room from dining room, one I'm sure I remember like a pillar, both sides free, but now to its right half filled with a broad white wall that is holed, like a small square tunnel, where logs are stored. It's clever, this, as you can fill it from the dining room and use it from this side. My father probably put it in. He was smart like that. The fireplace is large and stone, an oval frame in its centre in which there's no picture but there should be, of a lady, I always think. Below it, probably to my family's chagrin, I'm building a montage of polaroid pictures taken over decades; they mark the voyage of my children's growth and mine and my friends and their children. It's beautiful. It's the thing that guests stop and stare at, point if they're in it, find themselves, remember and feel all that sweetness that comes with a happy past. To the left of where I sit on the huge, ancient sofa is the wall that faces the glass doors to the terrace. There used to be one large painting there by an artist who lived with us, Tom Pomfret, I can't quite remember it now but I think it contained boats and was a landscape. There are dozens of Tom's paintings all over this house and also in London in the house in which I grew up. Tom lived in the basement there, at the other end from the flat, and he was large and funny and wore pink earrings at Christmas. He never sold much despite the many exhibitions we held for him, me shoving plates of cocktail sausages up at guests spilling drinks in the basement corridor, Tom morose the next day. Not enough red dots. He'd make marmalade with the housekeeper and bitch at the kitchen table and treat us with chocolate biscuits, and out here, where he'd come with us at Easter, he'd bake rum baba and throw coins in the pool to make us learn how to swim. I still have the rum baba moulds he used. I can't throw them away. But his painting from the large wall is gone and replaced by thirty-six framed pieces of a Japanese tapestry that was once one piece. It used to hang in the drawing room in London. It was what my father left to me in his will. My home in England doesn't have a wall big enough so I brought it out here and reluctantly moved Tom's painting. But other than that, this room is the same; the rugs, the fireplace, the long window at the back, even the curtains that hang at the tall glass doors. We used to do shows in here, Annie Get Your Gun and anything Judy Garland. Often a quick barbershop quartet to the ranks of parents forced to move the sofa so that the split level became a stage, and then forced to sit on the uncomfortable wicker bench at the end. I split my head on that step one night of being chased with a wet dishcloth by my brother, spinning around this circular house, a foot slip and crash, my mother hurried from the vegetable patch where she'd been collecting tomatoes in a storm while dressed entirely for going out to dinner. I remember lying on her lap as my father drove, her hand bright red to my head, how the doctor said it was like a tiger's claw had got me, how the waiting room was filled with campers nursing broken ankles, plastic bags over casts, tent wires that had tripped them in the rain.

SAMSON

I want to write about Samson, my dog, who is dead, his body anyway, who died almost a year ago, who I miss, we all do, who is still so alive in my head. He died last October after a failure of his kidneys brought on by something he ate many months before which brought him low at the time but I ignored it, as is my get-on-with-it survival want that I seem to apply to everyone, including myself, in my care. My dependents have to be pretty bad to warrant a trip to the hospital, or even over-the-counter medicine. Mostly I figure it out myself, my children patched up with sweating it out or magic gel or hot broth and sleep. It's mostly worked apart from the week-long episode of poorly dog six months before he died when I was certain he'd eaten a rotten rat and just had to pull himself together. I didn't know such a thing could get into his kidneys, the pulling together cause an irreparable strain that would emerge later as vomiting, a terrible foul breath that was, the vet told me, the toxins that he could no longer process. We'd taken him to have his teeth cleaned. They did a blood test. The news came in a phone call while I was busy doing something else. He was born in my hands, pushed out of his whippet mother as she circled by the Aga, I broke the seal on his sac. He was supposed to go to my friend and his identical brother to stay with me, but they determined the switch, the whippet twins, and he stayed instead. He put up with my tough love, he forgave and loved relentlessly, when we would go away for long summers here, leaving him at home with a friend come to stay, we would sing the going away song, *No Samson, no cry,* and we would cry a little and our hearts would lurch a lot. He was our boy. His last days were a trip to Scotland, ten hours in a car, stinking and forgiven for it though I didn't yet know he was ill. And when the phone call came from the vet and I stopped what I was doing, she said, *It's better sooner than later,* and so I called my children home. He died in our arms, those eyes that knew, he knew it was time to go. We buried him in open air in the arms of the great juniper tree high up in the woods where only we would know. My son returned to the place three months later to find his body picked clean, a perfect skeleton of Samson, the tilt of his whippet head. He has taken his skull. And people come to the farm and say they thought they saw a whippet running in the fields, chasing deer, and we sing the song of him and cry.

THREE JOURNEYS
THROUGH FRANCE

We would be taken by Daimler, a chauffeur in uniform, to Victoria Station, my siblings and mother, a housekeeper and I, to begin our journey to France. That was in the early days before my mother took to driving herself. The train to the port, exciting! We were off to the place I loved best. My mother's sandwiches, hard and uninviting. The ferry, excruciating and vomitous, how awful the stink of puke in the rocking toilets, doors swinging, a tiny cabin or seats on deck, I would always hurl over the side. The train to Paris, exciting again! The Paris metro, terrifying, my mother shoving limp tickets in our hands, the barriers snapping our legs, my sister's suitcase always too large to fit. Running for the sleeper, the train just caught and all night to love the journey south, heaven! Unless, due to less of us, my mother's refusal to buy the sixth bunk brought a large and stinking Frenchman in to watch us change our knickers under sheets. But the sleep, the lovely hurtle and gentle drift into night broken only by the snap of the blinds as morning released a sudden change in view. The earth! Red, the window open, the smell of pines, and our father there to meet us. And then it changed, the trains forgotten, the chauffeur and Daimler replaced by a Citroën with my mother at the wheel. She hated motorways, the blur, the paege, the driver's seat on the wrong side. She loved maps and A-roads and Romanesque churches. We would go to Chartres, that spire appearing over flat fields. We would stop in Cluny and press our faces to the railings of the grand stables. We would crash. One summer an overturned coach shut the motorway sending everyone onto our route, it was raining, we were late, the hotel gave away our rooms. We slept in a car park next to a church whose bells rang out every hour as did the car horn due to my mother's legs which were looped through the steering wheel, the only place to put them. I slept on the green suitcases in the boot, the same place I was the next day when she dozed off on a mountain road and hit another car head on. I flew to the front. We survived, the headlights didn't, the last of that twisting tarmac done in black. How different from my father who was never late, never hurried, never left anything to chance. Every summer he would pick one of us to be his companion on a very different journey south, myrtle cakes at motorway service stations, a detour through Switzerland playing spies in expensive hotels, his Porsche serviced and clean. We would arrive with my mother like survivors of a blizzard, he would greet us in ironed shorts, not a hair out of place, the lucky person smiling with him, never me.

DEATH ON THE ROCKS

They were piled on the rocks, fifty or more, a spread of jellyfish cradled in stone, their little pulsing bodies translucent against grit, we could see sand through them. They glistened, stranded, we thought they'd been washed up, one enormous wave that took them there, how else could they have arrived in such a pile, gathered in drowning, the sun bleaching them into nothing, whatever becomes of a jellyfish once all the seawater and jelly is gone. We stood over them wondering how to put them back without hurting them, without them hurting more. I'd read recently of a boy who could pick them up with his hands, something confident as with nettles, but I didn't remember how. We thought about buckets and spades, maybe we could save some. And then we saw the children with sticks and the mother pointing and the father standing guard, his green shorts belted, his legs and glasses firmly planted, his grey hair to the neck, arms folded, face set. We saw how his children stood at the water's edge, their spears lifted, how they stabbed at the sea and shouted. How they carried each méduse dripping from the waves, its tendrils hanging, how they threw them to the outcrop of jagged edge and heat. We walked away saying, *How can people do that?* and I thought of all the times I'd said silence is complicity. I turned back. My children said afterwards my French is fluent when I'm angry. I think I was more upset, but they can have their story. They were watching. I was in it, this contretemps on the beach, sunshine and parasols, a sparkling air which started with *Excusez-moi, monsieur, ce n'est pas bien de tuer des méduses comme ça* but I never got the chance to say the next bit, *s'ils sont là on ne nage pas* because the fury from monsieur green shorts, glasses, grey hair to the neck was instant. The words had hardly left my mouth. It was as if he was expecting them. Both barrels at me: he was on holiday; he could do what he liked. He arched and leered and took two steps back and opened his arms and raised his voice and people turned on their towels, looking over bronzed shoulders, and I said I was free to speak. Of course I walked away, that big man with his children taught gleefully to kill, that they have more right than another, their dominion assured by the stance of their father, the collusion of their mother. I only had to say my piece. Know that I had said it. I thought later, he's in pain to be able to watch so stonily those jellyfish pulsing quietly to their death on the rocks. He doesn't realise we're one. Les méduses will return. There are more of them. His children will pay.

MY LOGICAL SON

M y son thinks I should write these the day before and activate some sort of automatic timed post for first thing in the morning so that they drop into your inboxes when you wake up. He reckons people prefer that and also more people will get to them, it being the habit of most of us to pick up our phones and see what's what before the day's begun. Which is true. Except for this, that a whole lot of you are waking up now, you being in America and not Europe, and also I'm on holiday, a decision made on the Eurostar where I said I'd post any time I liked. Also, something else. If I was as organised and logical as he's suggesting, I'd have a piece of writing hovering with one foot out the door each evening and I'd think about it, I wouldn't be able to cope. These pieces stay with me even after I publish, it's only the shunt of tomorrow that pushes today beyond reach. I'd go back and change it if it hadn't already gone the moment I get that feeling, *finished*, that sense in my blood that this is it. Because here's the thing. Even the words I imagine I'll write while making my coffee to bring up and drink while I type, even those words so close to the actual and which seem so perfect while the kettle boils are often not the ones that get first dibs by the time I've gone upstairs to sit at my desk. Others have arrived that I wasn't expecting. The point is immediacy, the white-knuckle ride of not planning and not knowing what I'm going to say or how I'm going to say it, how it will continue or how it will end, and not being able to think or go back, not be tempted to change a thing. Not a single word. Like this. And how I feel this evening will not be what I want to say tomorrow. But rest assured, my son, when we get back to the UK I'm going to start the early morning routine again, it being the only time I can write these posts once normal work resumes, and you will say, *Why are you always so tired?* except you won't because you'll be in Armenia. You'll read these over lunch unless you can sneak them into morning class, you won't get them first thing no matter how early I get up. And the house will be quieter without you. And I will miss your logic and I will miss you. And I'll probably write about that.

LES AUMARETS LOVES YOU

J ust now I saw the cat's face in a pile of clothing on the
floor. Not the actual cat, she's in England but this often
happens when we're on our way home, or rather back to that
other home, or returning from anywhere having been away
a long time. She thinks of us, she transports herself in that
clever cat way, her face appears and I think *ah, yes, Kenny*.
Now I know what you're thinking: *idiot*, but here's the thing.
However reasonable it might be to assume that the actual
explanation lies within my head I've spent a lifetime being told
I'm a fool so it no longer matters. Kenny knows we're coming
home and that's that. Through space and time, for which she
gives little shrift, she's projected herself to let me know that
inside that furry little head she's on to us. We're leaving. Not
today but soon. And so begins the prowl about this house,
gathering things spread out through summer. There's a bowl
of sunglasses on the dining room table I must sort through
and decide which ones can be left out for guests. I've already
done the hats, they're balanced on a bust of my father in the
hall, my own put away in a cupboard which will lock with all
the other bits of mine that I want kept safe. Summer dresses,
bikinis, the Polaroid camera, my straw bag and a spare pair of

flipflops. My niece is coming, and after her my sister-in-law. Ronnie Barker used to rent this house; his summer holidays spent exactly like ours. Have I mentioned that? And there were others, too, other families for whom this is just as much a home on repeat, a summer retreat, who've loved it as much as we do. I often think of them, like the fourth dimension Spaniards except completely unaware of us who will leave and leave little trace. Like Ronnie Barker who would wake up in my bed, pull back the curtains on that glorious view, curse at the handle that always falls off, learn to do it gently. They come and inhabit and imagine it's theirs which it is for those weeks, a gentle padding about these stone floors, a terrace chair sat in every year, a favourite spot around the pool. This house with its mighty heart. Les Aumarets loves you.

PEOPLE ARE READING

I finished my book (the butler did it) and we stretch this last day into all of our favourites bits: coffee in bed, the curtains pulled back on a view that takes in the far hills. A set of tennis before it gets too hot (I lost). A breakfast of green juice, croissants for the kids. There's always some admin, we did it, I swam, made lunch of leftovers and ate while playing backgammon (I beat him in spectacular fashion, the win of the summer, I couldn't play again our normal best of three, the after-quiver was too much for me). And then I finished my book by the pool, reading quickly, sometimes it has to be done even with an Agatha Christie, the pages ancient and falling out, the cover stained and peeling. And now here, the last post of the summer, not that it won't be summer in England but in England I get back to work on a novel I hope and pray and wish and will do practically anything for to get over the line and bought and published because I know and my agent knows it's a damned fine idea and incredibly it hasn't been done before. So keep your fingers and toes crossed for me people, it's a tough publishing world out there and don't I know it. But that is for Monday and this is today, our last day here. It's been fun writing these – thanks for reading by the way, have I said that? Thanks so much for reading. It never ceases to amaze me that these minutiae are interesting or be a mystery which strike home and which wander off unnoticed. I've had to stay cool on the roller coaster of being praised and ignored, it's been good for me. It occurred to me the other day as the carriage took another hurtling rise and dip that I'd better get used to it, these posts which have become a habit have no end in sight; I might carry them on forever. Why not? That's the beauty of this place built for writers, we can gabble and be read and it no longer feels as if I'm shouting into the void. People are reading. Hooray! You save me.

TIME

I need to make friends with time. I was thinking this as I left the house, how quickly the summer has gone, how quickly this life is going, the bits I love and even now the bits I don't love so much don't seem to drag so much as they did when I was young. The whole thing has speeded up, as is the cry of everyone over whatever age it is when summers do not go on forever. I need to make friends with time, this out-of-control aspect that drives us, that consumes me. It's happening after all. It's with me all the time. And that's the thing – *all the time* – this is how I've come to understand it. I made the mistake once of saying to my sister, *Time doesn't exist.* What I meant was, *As you perceive it,* but it was lost in a shower of ridicule, such an easy stab. What I mean is that time as I know it is a block through which I move, it's not time that moves at all but me, the space that is me. And for some reason that I'm sure someone reading this will explain, as I get older I experience my travel speed up. But time itself hasn't done a thing, it's not responsible for this feeling, it, as Ian Banks observed when a character looked into the eyes of the universe, has no emotion. All of my yesterdays and all of my tomorrows are co-existing, these echoes of me can, in certain lights, be seen in that tracing paper plane. But my attachment, oh boy that's the trouble, that's why it's so hard to be friends. Not wanting moments to end, thinking time's a thief, has it in for me, unable to fathom that time doesn't know I exist let alone know my name, that more love and beauty are right around the corner. I have this when I leave the house, too frightened to presume I'll be back again in case my presumption thwarts me. As if time were vindictive I say goodbye as if it were forever. As I was leaving I saw the angel. I said, *How you doing?* and it replied, *Just preparing for your death.* This shook me – you can imagine – until it explained each change is a death to the greater spheres, it's no big deal, just stepping through a doorway. And one day when I'm a hundred and one I will die in the way we know it and that moment exists already as clearly as this one, on the Eurostar, leaving Paris for London. And I am walking back into the house in winter in France, a ten-day sortie in December. That exists too.

HOME TO THE AGA

Home. Sad. New chapter. A long day's travel from France made longer by my insistence we go by train. Andy says he'd let his EasyJet go toe to toe with my Aga in front of George Monbiot any day of the week but I'm not giving in. It's twice the price and double the journey time and I'll do it again next year for the effort of not contributing to CO_2 emissions another drop as far as I can help it, which doesn't include my Aga and already I can see him smirking and saying, *I see.* Don't we all make these choices, choose which hills to die on? I'll give it up one day, of course I will, it's obviously unsustainable, unjustifiable, I get it. Also its quiet, steady breathing, its body of few parts, its constant warmth give me comfort in ways only other Aga lovers will understand. He didn't grow up with one. He hasn't lived with one for thirty years. Yes, we've had the conversation about buying a new electric or converting it to wood-fuelled and no I won't be doing either of those things. Electric ones are not the same, they're like decaf coffee or fat-free milk; either do it properly or don't do it at all. And wood fuelled I don't have time for. So it's the real thing or nothing, my ancient oil-fuelled beast or that bloody electric range with super sleek induction hob that he adores that's beautiful and efficient and can boil milk in ten seconds and drives me mad with its lack of knobs. Where's the on switch? What if I want to keep something warm? How do I lean against it in winter? I come home to the Aga, I dry clothes on it, I know how to cook on it, I have all those Aga burns up my arms from taking things out of the oven. It brings me happiness. He doesn't understand how sad I would be, not just a bit sad but sad like something missing. So I pay double the price and travel twice as long, I plant 80 hectares of new woodland, I let my garden run wild, I compost leftovers, reuse silver foil, wash out freezer bags, nurture insects, reduce plastic packaging, rarely buy new clothes, mend and make do over and over again and I keep my Aga. George Monbiot's welcome to get in touch.

TOUCHING THE VOID

I didn't know what I was going to write about today but it wasn't this. A friend just messaged with some terrible news. It's too soon to talk about it, but I will talk about the other times it's happened to people close to me: a friend's son who took his life when he was only nineteen, and another close friend who'd been unravelled by a *Get Well Quick* weekend workshop of the kind that would be hauled up for malpractice if the system was regulated which it isn't. I didn't see it coming those times either. I suppose one never does, or rarely; those who really want to die do it quietly, with intent. They don't tell anyone. They don't let anyone talk them out of it. I have another friend who's often got his feet over the ledge. I say to him, *Do me a favour, if you want to die, fine, but sweet Jesus let me know. I promise I won't talk you out of it. It's the shock that kills.* It's the shock that kills, not the person who's jumped or tied or cut or swallowed, they've already chosen their way out, but for the rest of us it's a nail bomb going off in our lives, we're not prepared, we haven't a chance to seek shelter. It's a rip in the fabric of time and space, it cannot be mended. I've been in the place where it seems impossible to go on. I know how calm and convincing the eye of that storm is. I'm clear that no one jumps or ties or cuts or swallows in order to cause more pain, it's the goddamn pain they want to stop. But consider this, if you're considering it, there's no guarantee it will stop on the other side of that door and I can guarantee if you don't let us know it won't for those around you, who love you, who wish beyond heaven that you'd come back. Your pain is terrible but I don't mind. I'd stand beside you a thousand times over rather than wish you gone. Do you remember that scene in *Touching the Void* when he's fallen on the ledge, his leg broken, the rope cut? Below him the chasm drops into blackness and he realises two things: one, if he stays on the ledge he'll die, and two, if he goes down further he might live. It was the knowledge of that choice which saved him.

WHEN I'M CLEANING
WINDOWS

S o this happened:

Hi Eleanor, it's XXXXX here. I started cleaning your windows today but ultimately didn't finish. I'll be honest and completely straight to the point with you. I don't feel comfortable cleaning your windows anymore.

Something strange happened the last time I cleaned your windows inside, especially going in the loft and it's started happening outside as well now. I won't go into great detail but whenever I'm around your house I feel extremely uncomfortable and feel a strong presence that I cannot explain that doesn't want me there.

I'm one of XXXXXXX and therefore I believe in forces both of good and bad and I strongly feel that I do not want to be around the property because of the aforementioned reasons.

I have enjoyed cleaning your windows over the years but I believe it's ultimately to a detriment if I continue cleaning your windows. I thank you for your custom over the years and I wish you well.

And it happened at the end of a long day which began at 4am so I'm pretty tired. What to make of it? The second load of X's cover the name of a religious sect, but I've blocked it out because which religion and which sect is not the point. The issue is this: over the last thirty years of living in this ancient place, wisteria dripping at the door, I've experienced the reporting of these shadow lands; whichever way you want to phrase it, I've heard it all before. If you've read the memoir you'll know I've torn down buildings to try and assuage the haunted feeling people have periodically brought to my table, convinced they've tapped into a trouble of which I was unaware. I would have picked this up and run with it too if it hadn't dawned on me some years ago that what they're feeling has nothing to do with my home and everything to do with them. This place stirs things up, that much I do know, and I've seen its effects again and again projected into a story of wrong that exists outside of them, a place they can blame and remain blameless. Good luck my friend the window cleaner, frightened of the darkness within. You carry those forces with you.

SPARK

It's been a long day. There's going to be a lot of that now that I'm back in England. I was up at five to get to London by seven so that I could find three hours of quiet working time in a cafe before going to lie on the treatment bed of my magic friend with her magic hands which do what they do regardless of whether she's in charge. *I just make it up,* she'll laugh, which is code for something greater happening; she is one of life's master healers. There. I've said it. On the way to the cafe I passed a woman on the street who sat in her raincoat, hood up, a stub of a roll-up cigarette in her fingers. I doubled back and asked if I could get her a coffee. She nodded. Milk and sugar? Another nod. I noted in myself the urge to not give her sugar. Can you imagine? A well-healed middle-aged woman lecturing a woman on the street about the benefits of healthy eating. The front of it. The lack of understanding. Yoga and kale were not the issue. But it was her muteness that stayed with me as I walked away, fetched her a coffee and a croissant and delivered them back. She was there but not there. She was absent and in shock. I imagined myself in her shoes. Later I called Andy and we talked about it; he's retraining as a psychotherapist and works the free phone line of a therapy drop in, he regularly speaks to people for whom kale and yoga won't cut it. We talked about how society's set up to praise winners, reward success, how hard it is to do anything when the spark is gone and you're being blamed for it. We talked about the vitalness of connection. I'd driven up listening to *The Wild Edge of Sorrow* and told him about the town where heart disease skyrocketed as families fractured and community broke up. The science of belonging. I told him how when I left the cafe three hours later I walked past the woman again and this time she was writing, her anorak off, sun on her face, we locked eyes for a second and she flipped another page in her notebook. That spark of connection, her with the words she had written, that belonging that is the difference between life and death.

WINCHING HORSES

I'm editing, that delicate process of Jenga with words, this is the tweezer moment plus one big bit of heavy lifting. A whole chapter in which I cheated has to be un-cheated and done properly. All writers know how hard it is to keep momentum while moving through time. I want to say *and then it was April and this happened* and fill in those missing months with the past perfect tense which produces neither perfection nor tension. The live action is in the live action, being there; *she sat down* not *she had sat*. But it's so nerve-wracking, so hard to be present for every beat of the story, every pulse that those characters live through. I want to brush it over, get out the other side and yet of course, if I do, as I did, the reader misses the action too. The live pulsing beat of tension is lost. It's all in yawning retrospect. It will not do. So having gone through the easier little bits, a tweak here, a nudge there, I begin the dismantling of this end of act two from its cheating hindsight look back and rebuild it firmly in the now, the now of the novel, the next day. Did I say it was nerve-wracking? Also that terrible cut and paste when sections are put aside to be inserted somewhere else, that new file opened *CHAPTER 6 INSERTS* in which paragraphs are painstakingly lifted like rescued horses, their legs dangling, winched into the air and stabled temporarily in another yard while their stable is redesigned. I am flying the helicopter and controlling the winch and wielding the axe and using the chainsaw and holding the plans and taking the pencil from behind my ear and measuring the doors and pacing the walls and waving from the ground and leading the horses to their makeshift corral where they will not stay for long. I am doing all these things. And I will put it all back together. And it will be better.

GRIEF IS AN ANARCHIST

There is so much grief that I put it all in a hedge; a kilometre of vibrancy that my neighbours won the right to rip out, a deal struck with my back against the wall, it was that or court and a bill upwards of £200,000. They tantrumed enough to force a day in a lawyer's office, a mediation that cost us all a lot of money, their claim that their lives were threatened by the hedge's broad brush, its waving leaves, that they could not walk down the road safely in summer to get their right-wing newspapers. Really the problem was me, who they hate, my face made into a dartboard for all their woes including abandonment, loss and rejection. Never mind that it happened to them long before they moved to this part of the world, that they were hurt long before they left me. They have channelled it into a hedge as I channel my grief and come November, they swear they will send the bulldozers in, nothing will stop them. I have a champion in a friend and colleague who's won through charm and logic the ear of two of them, but one of them holds out, determined. It's heartbreaking that a hedge will fall foul of their pain, that vindictiveness for a suffering suffered long ago will find its way into chainsaws. It is the story of small minds and trauma and fury at a woman on a hill who won't bow to local dinner parties, who won't buy *The Telegraph* and agree all refugees are dirty. My hedge, it waves to me as I drive in and I say sorry every day. I'm sorry I couldn't save you. Maybe a miracle will happen.

WELCOME HOME

And so it begins. The voice in my head that gets me up at five in the morning and tells me to go and write. That voice has caused a lot of work to be done, many words on the page, short stories, whole novels, four of them, and all this. I've been looking back through the memoir and this diary, so much talking, so many stories and still they keep coming, that voice still finding a reason to send me to the kitchen table while the rest of the world sleeps. That's how they feel, these five am sorties, as if I am the only one awake in a snoring world. And my brain before it organises itself into what's important and what is not tumbles out this jumble of half-baked thoughts, the rubble and the leftovers and the not fully formed, the beginnings of a day. There is a silence unlike night. There is a quiet that I can pace through. This kitchen is a jumble of yesterdays; the washing-up liquid set down with the lid sprung open as a pan that is already put away was washed. A coat slung over the edge of a door by Andy who came in late, exhausted having spent four hours in Reading being locked out of his van. Kenny on the table spread out in post breakfast haze amongst fruit and water bottles. The chicken stock that I got going yesterday after dinner and which sat all night lidded and warmed on the hot plate of the rumbling Aga now put on the right-hand burner to slowly rumble itself into life and think about flavour. I notice it's waking a little too quickly while I sit here, I put coins beneath it to turn down the heat. And someone's got the knitting basket out, the needles last put away when Covid trickled out of our lives. Kenny raises her head to a distant shout of pipes or something further in the woods beyond, and satisfied the world isn't ending, goes back to sleep. And Percy comes in and claws at my leg, purring, saying, *Hungry.* And I have written five hundred words and it's time to stop.

BACK OF THE NET

We fell in love with the scorer of the Spanish team. I didn't catch her name in all the rush or see it on the back of her shirt but you know I'll look it up after I've posted this. She. Her. Of the magnificent feet and face and winning goal scored in the first thirty minutes of the first half. I'm not one for football and less one for nationalism and only moments like this, England in the World Cup, the Lionesses' roar, got me in front of the television with all the family, cheering, and hiding behind my hands on a Sunday morning in Surrey. And only in so much as we wanted England to win, those mighty women who've fought for female footballers to be taken seriously, given the same money, treated with the same respect as the men. And it really only lasted as long as it took for us all to fall in love with the Spanish player who celebrated with her shirt in her teeth so that Adidas would pay her what they owed her for smarting their brand all over the pitch. Did you know women's football was shut out until 19th January 1970, that a man landed on the moon before the FA committee voted to lift the ban on women playing professionally? Imagine the thinking behind that, the reasoning, because you can bet they came up with reasons. Oh yes we can't have our women who've just worked the munitions factories running about in shorts with their breasts jiggling about. Good God no. They might injure themselves. Back to the home, all of you. Fucking men in suits and excuse me if a man in a suit is reading this, you know who I'm talking about and I'm going to assume it's not you. All of these prejudices put into law against global majorities, what power play, did they never stop to think it couldn't last? Did they, in that boardroom in 1921, their ties loosened, their feet up, hear the echo of the lionesses' roar coming down the line, see their boots aimed? The Spanish won the World Cup. Women scored another goal.

SO MANY HATS

Nothing is more powerful than an idea whose time has come. I woke up with that in my head, or rather had it very early on spinning around as I drove in the morning light to ride my horse with friends before running home again in time to pick up my son to go circuit training. What a day it's been and it's not even three o'clock. I wear so many hats, swapping hour to hour sometimes, from mother to writer to the business of estates, emails coming in, checklists, things that need my attention right now. It started at five with mushroom coffee, my weaning from the real thing because I love it too much, and with it read an article Andy sent me about a woman whose mother planned her own end, meticulously, and how she unearthed the stories afterwards of her mother's life before she was born. It was those which made me think of the Victor Hugo quote, a quote I was going to use in the front of the novel I'm writing until I thought of a better one. I rode with my friends and told them the estate no longer welcomes fox hunting, a decision whose time had come, and they were sweet about it and said they understood. And then I sweated with my son over rowing machines and mountain climbers until he turned pale and I ate an apple.

We food-shopped on the way home, something with honey and tofu tonight, he wants to eat less meat, I agree. And I made a salad for lunch which he took so I made another one and another mushroom coffee which I brought to my desk to do some more winching of horses. Nerve-wracking! I know I always say that but get used to it. It always will be and I ever will. Lunch for the other two teenagers produced and here I am again, by way of an hour of admin, which I'll get back to after this, and phone call with a friend who I'm a bit worried about but he's a big boy and I said my piece. So many hats; estate meetings coming up that I must concentrate on, an edit to deliver, a teenager to deliver to Armenia. A list as long as my arm of things I must do and after all that, there's that honey tofu dinner to cook. And all I can think of is a bath and *The Road* which is bleak and I wish I could write like that.

THE SELFISHNESS OF LOVE

That friend I mentioned yesterday to whom I said my piece and about whom I worry. This is about recovery, addiction, sobriety. They've been in recovery for many years, in and out of it, and what it looks like to them, the terms they've come to with it, aren't what it might look like to another person, and I get that. They've found psychedelic avenues that present a benign version of escape. I have an opinion about that. I say fine. Me too. But here's the other opinion I have about their other choices, the not so psychedelic which was their downfall, which I hear still happens from time to time, and now they've met a person who is not in recovery at all. Far from it. The opposite of recovery. Lighting fires everywhere. Which you and I know is Lois Lane and kryptonite all rolled into one. Yet here's another ingredient to throw at this heady mix. Loneliness, of which my friend has suffered greatly. So they've met someone who lights their fires and keeps them warm and makes them shocked at their good fortune. They wrote to me and said, *Even as I write this it feels like a fiction*. They can't believe it, after all these years, someone is loving them. And they want it to last, and they want to care for this person with whom they have more in common than you can shake a stick at. Including a history of abuse, trauma and addiction. I read them the slow news riot act – *all addicts end up in one of four places: prison, hospital, sobriety or death. No exceptions.* They said, *Yes, I know,* and they do, better than most. They said, *I want to care for [this person].* I replied, *Then care for your sobriety.* And then I spoke about it later with Andy and he said, *If you gave them a choice – the loneliness they've suffered or six months of fire and falling off a cliff, which would they rather?* and it was a good question. They will find out and so will we and the selfishness of love, mine for them, my friend, sat up and sat down again.

THOUGHTS UNFINISHED

Gosh there's such a lot I can't write about here; the sticky ends of relationships, the interactions which throw me, the details I have to walk away with – this public diary is not the place for them. There would be betrayal. And hurt. There would be anger. And so I talk about what I'm having for lunch (yesterday's leftover salad augmented with half an avocado I found in the fridge and the rest of the smoked trout which needs eating). What I'm doing today (a thousand hats!). What makes my head hurt (the hats). What makes my heart hurt (my son going away). And I have imaginary arguments in my head about why I have to cook the dinner at lunchtime (there won't be time once we're back from the orthodontist). And wonder who I'm arguing with (the kids are all in different places, Andy's at work, I'm in a pause between rushing in and rushing out). One of my favourite David Shrigley pieces is his tombstone list. It sums me up, these frantic marks which signpost my day from dawn until late tonight. Bread Milk Cornflakes Baked Beans Tomatoes Aspirin Biscuits *dead.* That'll be me. And in the meantime, I get all sorts of things done, an edit finished yesterday, a bag packed and weighed and repacked and weighed again for Armenia, estate meetings prepped and arranged, appointments at the doctor and dentist, and near the end of this list I remember all the things I wanted to talk about today, how I had an interesting to and fro with someone recently about sobriety and what it means. They said they hadn't been an unmanageable drinker, just a glass of an evening, and I hadn't time to say this, what I wanted to say: that the distance between one drink and none, and a thousand drinks and none is the same. It's identical. You may as well drink a bottle as a glass. The tendrils of booze reach further than even I could have imagined and I have a pretty wild imagination. But the end has come so I promise I'll start with this seam tomorrow, and I leave with the thoughts unfinished, doctor, dentist, post office, printers *dead.*

THE ROAD

I finished *The Road* last night and I was prepared for its bleak but I wasn't prepared for its beauty. I read the last pages while my son got his braces fitted, another torture of sorts, I only half aware of his pain so lost in the pain of the boy and his father, their walk along the road. And then in the last pages I couldn't help but check how many I had left as the orthodontist in the far distance told my son to turn his head this way now and sorry for the bitter taste. The last paragraph came with the voiceover that he could get up, I couldn't stand it, the beauty of what was before me, how it ends, oh my god and my son shifting in his recline, his feet dropping to the floor, my finger on the final page, the orthodontist looking over, why did this mother not care. I cried without showing it, a moment's grace as they spoke to him a minute about aftercare and not eating sweets, what will happen if he doesn't clean them properly and I read the last lines again, just to be sure I hadn't missed something, to *do* it again, to be certain it's one of the finest endings I've ever read. And it was, is, I wasn't wrong, I hadn't misread in my hurry an art of such excellence that I want to hold the book to me like my son whose mouth is now a nest of metal, his speech relearnt to clamber over wire. I've left it on the kitchen table where I hope the Young People will pick it up. I told them over dinner it's about the end of the world. I'm not sure I did it justice. How could I? It has sat on my bookshelf for years, me walking past it, not daring, saying in my ignorance, *Oh god, really?* What an idiot. Read it if you haven't read it. Read it.

YOU'RE ALL I'VE GOT

It's all I've got. Said to me by a friend whose back's against the wall in every which way, who's running out of money, and time to become well when I said she could give up vaping. *It's all I've got.* I've become stern in my middle age. I don't waste time pussyfooting around with things I've got to say, however misguided, ignorant or harsh they might be. I'd rather be wrong than silent. That phrase is a tell, it's a great big red flag stuck in the ground. I used to say it about my three glasses of wine and three spliffs of an afternoon while the children had tech time. I was so lonely, so disconnected, so craving for that sweet spot of feeling something mattered. I didn't know, was completely oblivious to the fact that *it's all I've got* was standing in the way of having what I wanted. And here's another one – I've just done it inadvertently – the use of the possessive over an inanimate object, the thing I clung to as if it alone was saving me from drowning. *My wine. No one's going to take my wine away. It's all I've got.* If you've heard yourself say these phrases, and you're unhappy with your relationships – those with yourself, others, your life, the world consider putting down the thing that you're gripping like a baby with its comfort blanket and picking up that baby instead, the one that's in need of comfort. Pick it up for ninety days. Hold it every time it cries. Tell it you are always happy to see it. And if after ninety days you'd rather hold the blanket instead, then fine. You'll have learnt something.

TWO ARROWS

There were tears. Mine. They didn't look back, neither of them, Jacobi or Cat. Through security at Charles de Gaulle, we watched them go. Would he find his boarding pass? Would he remember to put his Important Documents holster back in position? Would he shut the zips? Cat, who he's travelling with, a first voyage for both of them, seemed to have it all sewn up. But then again I haven't spent sixteen years hovering over her, picking up behind her, making sure she's all right. Her mum and dad have done that and done it well. Their tears were at St Pancras where we took on the guardianship of both those arrows, to draw back in Paris, to let them fly. So we watched, Andy and I, soon just their outlines as his shorn peroxide head dipped and ducked, a strap over his shoulders, a phone replaced in a pocket as they turned to go. We saw them high five each other. We saw them not look back and this is as it should be. I gave myself the moments I needed to heave those sobs that say sixteen years, job done (for now). He'll be back for Christmas and next time he flies away it will be easier. The little child sitting on my knee, the cuddle up of blonde head, the comfort and the need is tucked inside him where he can always reach it. I will be there. And do you want to hear the best of it? Because he's a twin and as twins know, that relationship can have its ups and downs. I used to say, when they had their fights and wrangles and friendships that never seemed to be each other, *I wish for you to have each other's backs, whatever else you go through, that you're there when it's needed most* and that moment came as Jacobi was leaving, when he needed his brother most and his brother needed him. There were tears, theirs. It made my day. So I said goodbye and did look back at those sixteen years of growing in my arms, newborn to toddler to child to young adult; how does this magic work, how can it be understood that it passes in such a flash as they said it would, the mothers on the street who stopped me when I pushed that double buggy up a hill, exhausted, tearful, *Treasure this, it will be gone.*

TIME TRAVEL

When I was small, I was attacked by someone in a basement and it coloured my life a certain shade of hurt and anger familiar to people reading this. Life repeats itself, doesn't it, in ways that echo the original. A different stage, better lighting, costumes updated yet the theme remains the same. Attack from an outside source. Shouting into the void. Vulnerable. These neighbours that I've mentioned before, one of them even bears the same name just to drive the essence home in case I missed it in case I thought what is happening today was anything but a repeat of yesterday. It's an emotional flashback I'm in, a repetition in real time of something torturous that makes me freeze. I am alone. I am terrified. They, the neighbours, are just being shit cunts in their own shitcunty way that holds an essence of their own, meanwhile in my hurtle though time my Saturday night and Sunday morning have been splattered with the certain shades of hurt and anger that render me unable to see straight. That send me to the bunker, incapable of receiving even the most tentative of reaches. I made myself sit near Andy and let him stroke my back. Even that was difficult. I tried a hug but I couldn't do it. I'm aware a calmer, less frightened me would wish an end to the suffering and the causes of suffering to those unnameables whose houses I can see from my bedroom window but today I wish they'd meet terrific, terrible ends and be gone and all of this would stop as I wished it would stop long ago and wasn't heard.

MY FAVOURITE RUNNER

She wears milking trousers that stop short of the ankle, the kind I remember the herdsman in, and her top, a smock, is faded pink with collar standing proud like a vicar's without the slide of white cardboard. It's square like her trousers which are faded blue, stained with farmyard straw and farmhouse kitchen. From the back she's seventy at least, white ankle socks dusty and marked, goodness knows what shoes, I never get that far, so mesmerised am I by her form, but I imagine some sort of aged plimsole that's seen mud and rain and probably the stirrups of a well-worn saddle flung on a family pony. My favourite runner making her way along the lanes, a steady trot, grey hair flattened at the back, I won a wave and smile once as I passed, an arm raised, her crinkly face crinkled more. That time I'd followed her for almost a mile in my silent car, always I'm on my way training, to do what she does but with my favourite fireman in the backroom of the station that has tables pushed aside so I can sweat it out with burpees and weights. But her who looks like she's spent all morning in the milking parlour or mucking out the donkeys or baking fifteen different pies doesn't ask for kit and a room out of the rain or even a friendly fireman though I'm sure she'd get a kick out of what we do. I imagine her drying her hands on a dishcloth and thinking, *Time for my run* and without getting changed, without fancy shoes or breathable lycra or even a hair tie she's off, down the lanes, aged eighty or more, she's getting older in my mind as I type. I first thought when I saw her for the first time, *Really? At your age? Is there a point?* and promised myself I'd give up all this effort when I reached the stage of flattened hair at the back, but gradually I've got to know better. She's still running. She's still alive. And she waves her hand at me as I pass in my silent car.

BE GRATEFUL

The mystery book-sender strikes again; as in the sender is a mystery, not the genre of books which are nothing like whodunnits apart from the fact that I have no idea whodunnit. Or keeps doing it. The genre is as clear as the self-improvement on their shrouded face, "Let me help you!" they scream. "I'm too nervous to come out with it, so I'm going to send you nudges for do-at-home growth that I'm sure you'll thank me for one day. If I ever reveal myself. Which I won't because by the time you've reached enlightenment my smugness won't fit out the door." They're out there somewhere, this person convinced they've got my answers. They've been sending me books for years. The latest is by John O'Donohue, *To Bless the Space Between Us, A Book of Blessings* which I'm sure is delightful and good on you John for getting it together but I didn't *ask* for it. I didn't go on Amazon and spend $22 on a piece of non-fiction which will remind me in random open-anywhere nuggets to be grateful. How do you know I'm not grateful already Messrs Know-It-All Fixer? And why pick on me? It's the latest in a long line of unordered wellness packages delivered with no note and no sign of where they've come from. Given the many hundreds of people who've passed through these doors and lived on this land, narrowing it down to those who know my address won't quicken the search. One things for sure though, this doggedly determined person is certain that I need help. Maybe it's the window cleaner. Maybe it's any one of the faux spiritual smilers who've bowed their way across my kitchen. Maybe it's someone I've never met who's seen me lose my shit in the frozen peas aisle and decided to make me their project. "Expense be damned! I'm going to send this woman religiously biased tomes on How To Be A Better Person and I'm going to keep sending them to her until –" Until what? I ascend through a shower of Hail Marys? My star descends from the heavens? I turn blue or purple or gold or stop losing my shit in the frozen peas aisle? Maybe I should actually read one of them one day, there's enough to pick from piling up on my bookshelf in the bathroom and taking up valuable space. Perhaps I'll find some clue hidden between Daily Meditations and Breath Exercises. Maybe one day I'll be grateful for the hours of mystery my mystery book-sender has given me. I'm being facetious, you know I am, of course they're sweet and you're sweet and whoever you are, bless this space between us.

HORSE LOVE

He's called Tommy Shelby and Cillian Murphy doesn't have a patch on him. We went riding, or rather Blake and Sophie rode and I walked – I needed to see how they both were, neither of them had ridden for a while. It reminded me of when Blake and Jacobi were little, hours and hours on determined ponies, difficult to handle, the smaller they were the more headstrong, the less willing to behave. If you want to learn to ride, ride a Shetland, which they did, followed by tough little Welsh Bs and tiny draught cobs, no shoulder, their chests as wide as their behinds, easy to fall off, the saddles always slipping. It was with them through beating sunshine and pouring rain that my sons learnt the gift of horse love, now graduated onto actual horses, bigger and easier apart from having further to fall. But today it was Blake and Sophie, Jacobi being two and a half thousand miles away, and it was Tommy with Gully beside him, my friend's enormous war horse as gentle as a summer breeze. Last winter we spent two weeks riding in Patagonia, the high pampas, the mountains that towered, the turquoise seas that appeared when least expected. It was the rhythm of those hours, horse tempo, that entered our bones and slowed us down, our brainwaves aligning with the steady moves and I saw it again today. Two young people with much on their minds made quiet and easy, their expressions softened by a walk along a country lane, a view over the hedgerows, hands reaching out for blackberries. Gully and Tommy behaved admirably, like gentlemen mostly, their sweet eyes aware that on their backs were people regaining their horse legs. They're so wise, so wicked, so mighty. They cure everything. And I was reminded too, having read something by Sherman Alexie this morning about missing the community of co-workers, that the stables is where I get my chit-chat, my social in an otherwise solitary writer's world. And if there's no one to talk to I talk to Tommy. And he talks back. Does he ever. Oh boy.

THE PEOPLE ARE THE ART

The people are a work of art in this, the busiest room at the Klint & Mondrian, I'm at the Tate, this show closes tomorrow. *Tell me why it's your favourite,* a mother to a child, the mother excited by her daughter's interest, the child serious. Another says, *You're ruining everyone's enjoyment of the paintings,* this child sulky, who cares about the paint, this place, I want to go home. Pushed buggies seeking with wheels a way through. Kneeling in wide skirts to toddlers to explain the context of the First World War. Beautiful people, this art world space that reaffirms my faith in human nature, that there are so many who'd flock on a Wednesday afternoon to see these paintings, to care to walk slowly, to take it all in, try and understand, drink it. A woman with flame hair, red out of a tube like the paint, and her friend small and mouse, *Do you want to go to the roof for a sneaky glass of wine to talk about it?* as they paused in the doorway, the show almost done. A young, floppy curls Adonis and his mythical lover, arms about shoulders, slim hips, photographed in front of a large pastel curly flower by his sister perhaps, his proud mother, a sculptural face, a headscarf, smiling at her shoulder. A woman with talking-point glasses, orange and thick-rimmed.

A boy with dragons etched into his jeans. Colourful trainers and psychedelic skirts over jeans. A blonde moustache on a young man's face worn with awareness and John Lennon glasses. Head-turning elegance in a woman all in white, pink boots. And the work on the walls? How Klint swirls, how Mondrian orders, it's a clever curation, I'm not sure we all bother to read all the words that inform, I never do, or rarely, I want the artist to speak not the person who thought long and hard how to hang it. I can't walk in order when I arrive, I have to walk through, double back, pass by, let it wash over me, swim in it, arrive somewhere like here, a bench in the last room where I can watch paintings and people interact. I always get waylaid by the moving art, distracted by it, I wonder what this place would be like without people, how would I receive the art differently, would I enjoy more or less. The Tate is my church, one of them, any altar to art will do. It's where I see sacrifice and god, it's where I am replenished. And the comfort in this crowded place that I am not alone. The care in the air. It's palpable. Magnificent. Like the paint. Like the people who walk by.

BADGERS MARRYING
LAMPPOSTS

For the day when our sexual organs mean nothing more than that, no implication other than their ability to do what they were made to do. For the day when leaning into your own special mix of feminine and masculine is as daily as breathing and as unremarkable. Sophie asked me on the way back from seeing *Barbie* why is it that kids take it out on their mums – a line in the movie she was seeing for the second time because I wanted to see it. I said, *Okay prepare yourself for the most broad brush of gender sweeps but it's for a couple of reasons: mothers are safer and fathers are cowards.* Whoa whoa there. Harsh! I know. Sorry. I'll put it another way, although is there another way to put it? Because these roles are begun in the cradle and they are roles. Mothers are softer on their sons, they let them get off light, they don't teach them how to be disliked. Girls are told to be dependable; they're taught to stay at home. It sparked a conversation about the differences between men and women in which we kept having to return to that premise, limited yet necessary, that men are like this and women are like that, in order to have the conversation. It doesn't make sense if you break it down yet without it we get sidetracked into the also truth of the myriad variations and exceptions to the rule. Of course there's no such thing as men and women, and of course there is. So I said, *Here comes the nonsensical broad brush again: in my experience men are more sensitive and women are tougher.* And that was taught in the womb, too. So, for the day when those terms are as meaningless as the colour of our eyes, and as useful for conversations about eye colour and nothing else. What name I give myself an annotation in the big book of what it is to be a woman. There's a line in the novel I've just handed in, one character says to another, *Every time you are yourself you widen the definition of what it is to be that thing,* and this gets to the heart of what I mean. To shake off these constructs, this straight jacket. I want to dive into the hysteria and say, *Everyone relax. It doesn't matter.* Blake in the back said, *They're so frightened,* and it comes to that, that if we stop this clinging the world will end and badgers will marry lampposts. But they won't. And the world won't end. Nothing will happen. That which we are will carry on as it always has minus the violence and rage and stifling and condemnation and we will be happier.

SERVICE GAMES

My favourite games were Scullery Maid, Queen, and Ferryman. All of them in service. For Scullery Maid I polished for hours the silver, gathered from about the house in my small arms and taken to the basement on a tray along with my copper coin collection, a huge jar tipped out on the big chest freezer in the ticking laundry room, the wooden rack heavy with drying clothes, the rope holding it fast out of reach. I drew the ironing stool up to the white wall, my small legs put aside to get close, the chest lid spread with copies of *The Guardian* to keep it clean of *Brasso*. How I worked. Under threat of an unnamed mistress – they were in charge, they were mean, I was the lowest of the low – I bent over my chore, my fingers sticky as the silver and copper shone. I would feel the duress of it. I would wipe my brow and wonder at my fate. The silver shining and arranged on a tray, the coppers left behind, I carried it to the dining room where The Queen lay asleep on the back of the brown sofa. She was oblivious to the servants who kept me down, none of this was her fault. Woken but not cross, her head raised to watch, I laid the silver about her, covering the sofa, balancing a jug, a tankard, a small oddly shaped platter around her tabby body. Her tail was curled neatly. She approved and blinked slowly. She smiled her tabby smile. These were my acts of my devotion, My Queen who deserved daily worship, whose beauty the stars bowed down to. And the blue walls made her regal and the windows smeared London grime against trees and the Duke of Argyll glared with stony eyes from beneath his wig and she closed her eyes and rested. I took my skateboard from its lean beside the umbrellas in the hall. Outside, a different tempo altogether. The heavy front door I closed quietly, my jeans already old, I held the railings at one end of the street and announced, in a cap I wasn't wearing, that the ferry was leaving. The sound of the docklands loud in a silent leafy street. Horns of ships blaring and at my feet the queues of harried ant families. Fathers in bowler hats, mothers holding children, older ones linking to younger, suitcases held four a piece. They crowded aboard; they were going on holiday among the regular work crowd who did this journey daily. And we were off, my hands grabbing black iron railings, the skateboard clattering over paving stones, the sound of it as my palms turned black, I kept my feet still in case to crush them. *Rattle-rattle* hard plastic wheels across uneven slabs, a father grabbed by a mother, her face a panic, the father stoic weighed down by the weight to be calm. The suitcases under his arms almost falling, children clinging on and screaming as the waves crashed, half excitement half fear. My fingers around the moulded black spears that kept the garden away from the street, reaching for the next and the next, the evergreen hedge of tiny leaves poking through, brushing my body, I kept close in to let the nannies pulling children home from kindergarten pass. By the end of the day I had ferried those ants, the ant families and workers from one end to the other fifty times, such hard work, no boats had sunk, no one fallen overboard, everyone delivered safely. And my hands were black with London dirt and I stained the walls coming in, dragging my fingers across paintwork.

YOUR OS HAS BEEN UPGRADED

Imagine. A bank of screens, we're leaning over one, fascinated by what's going on, a group of us. We watch each other's progress and today, this minute, it's mine that's interesting. *How's she doing? Has the new algorithm taken?* The avatar that is me at this kitchen table, typing, this system that is running, is being watched over. The normal thing happens, I'm triggered by an email sent in good faith that comes back as a public correction, the spider's web lines are twanged and up comes the critic ready with answers: *it's because you're stupid, you're really an embarrassment, they're definitely laughing at you, they think you're a fool! You've revealed your soft underbelly. They're going to attack you.* And we're off on the merry-go-round of feeling shit but no, hang on, something's changed. We lean into the bank of computers and watch. *I'm sorry,* I say to the critic. *But we don't run those scripts anymore. The OS has been upgraded.* And I say it again and again. When shame rears in many guises. When panic sets in. When catastrophisation takes a hold and *I'll always be a failure* gets its feet under the table. When the fixer turns up. When the slave girl gets ready. When ugly is a sure thing and old is a disaster. *I'm sorry, we don't run those scripts anymore.* It's an odd sensation because it's true and it works. Sometimes I say, *I get that you want to run it, but even if I could it wouldn't function like it used to,* and I sympathise with the critic's dejection. And when it proffers the old floppy disc with *rubbish* written in magic marker on the label but finds there's nowhere to put it, or the programmes that used to spring into action at the tap of a button come up with the spinning wheel of rainbow patience followed by a pop up saying, *No,* I stand by and feel the critic's pain. Sorry for itself and getting smaller each time, I watch it wander off with its arms full of hard drives and dongles and old wires cut off at the neck. It has nowhere to put them. Nothing fits anymore. We each have our own way of making this system work, the language, the tricks, the imagination, the vision. I love this for its simplicity. I see a bank of computers, a lighted room, laughter and interest and a group of us leaning in. I see upgrades and bug fixes and system improvements and an avatar that is me, typing at this kitchen table.

SYMPATHY FOR THE DEVIL

I was planning on talking about needles before I started cleaning out the medicine drawer. Then there they were, not exactly the kind I used to use, but near enough to give me a jolt. The same plastic wrapping the way they used to come out of the vending machine at the hospital. Not a vending machine but you know what I mean, or perhaps you don't; we use to stop by and pick up new fits from a box outside, a clean needle exchange, nothing's every really clean with needles. My body would know before I did, the shake that was coming, it would curl into itself, quake, I'd feel sick, my hands would rattle. That journey home with our supplies was filled with dread and excitement. There was such subterfuge to it, we'd clear the decks, curtains closed, shutters drawn, friends we might have seen on the way turned down, a rush to get started, possessions scattered. Always sitting on the floor, I don't know why, perhaps nearer to drop something, less far to fall. Not that what I was using was drowsy. It was the opposite, crystal meth, a day and night ahead of me of writing so intense my legs would swell. But I want to talk about the process, I want to get into it because I'd watch it so keenly when I was learning and I'd do it so expertly once I'd learnt. I was good at it. The reassuring packaging, the sterile water and not so sterile spoon. How much, always a guess and a risk, a shake and tap of fragile plastic, a lip to knock back. A burn and soak into cotton wool balled up so small it would filter, the belt or tie or thin rope around my arm, alternating, I was ambidextrous. The press of clean sharp, the drawback of blood, the push of that precious liquid my body knew was coming, it was as if time stood still. I was interrupted once at that moment, a *cooee!* knock on the door and a scramble, hiding things, furious inside, outside pretending. *Go away,* I thought while keeping it snappy enough to dispel long conversation, certain I'd tricked her, my friend, that she'd walk away without a clue and not think, *Huh.* It ruined the moment. I had to start again. Because the high begins at first planning *shall we have a taste?* And the having it – that flick-flick on the upright hard body, the air bubble knocked out, the safety measures so acute for something so broadly dangerous, the finding the vein, that sharp intense pain, the everything stopped in my throat – that is only a part of it. When I see a needle in the medicine drawer I remember the all-consuming hunger, how it eclipsed and narrowed hurt to a single prick of light so intense that life became dark around it. I remember the years lost. I remember the why, the point.

PERFECT

The trouble with you is that you're just too perfect. So said my father to my sibling again and again. A lifetime of hearing that will render you useless at being flawed, which we all are, we which all essentially have to be. What a weight to carry. What a terrible permanence. I escaped that sentence but I heard it. The impact was felt. The inference that the rest of us weren't was experienced as a flaw in itself, the greatest one, the one that encompasses. I didn't know it was a gift to have it pointed out that I was human. I determined not to be. I determined to be like my sibling. To not be human is a hell of a game to play here, partly because I've always felt I was visiting and partly because the visiting me is undeniably flesh and blood, and the point of all this flesh and blood is to be it in all its oozing uncomfortable mess, to be vulnerable utterly so that life – and by that, I mean safety – comes down to relationships, the universe experiencing itself. So to play the double game, be not human, be this machine who doesn't feel, does nothing wrong, gets everything right, never lets the beauty in to make them cry is a sort of loss-loss on a grand scale. I used to work on it with my therapist. *Do you believe you're human?* she asked. *Not really,* I replied feeling smug.

And she didn't mean the time I lay on a rock by a quarry lake tripping on mushrooms and seeing myself in my true guise, at my true size, the wonder when a friend shouted it was time to go, that I had to fit all that into this tiny body, and my reply didn't mean that either. I was talking about the barrier to being part of this chaotic scramble, an ant on the face of a planet, one of millions, the same as everyone else. You know how it is with addicts, you're either king of the world or a piece of shit and there is no in-between. The normal lands of even keel, no drama, a mediocre existence where some things go right and some things go wrong and both are fine is anathema. It is too vulnerable. The trouble with my father was that he was just too oblivious. The damage of those words, the perfectionism worm sent to burrow, caused pain and suffering unknown. This, that I do every day is an antidote, one of many I take, a draught of pressing *publish* when I know it can't be perfect, when I don't know if it's finished or not.

ON THE ROAD

Traffic jam. Early morning. Sunrise. Stuck in my car on the A3 at 6am and google maps has gone red line on the road, it's not far but there's no getting out. An accident probably. I often think when this happens, a slip of time, if I'd left moments earlier would that have been me, because it's someone like me who woke to an alarm at 4am or near enough, who stumbled out the rituals of their getting up, made coffee and green juice, packed their bag, fed the cat, had a shower or not. They drove away like me checking with their left arm behind them that they had remembered their work bag, yes, I can feel it, hands back on the steering wheel, and did I remember my laptop, phone, glasses. Did they stop and check? Go back to reaffirm they'd locked the door, shut the windows, turned off the light. Did they leave someone sleeping beside them? The sky turns pink, strips of clouds, a seagull calls, the lights of the cars in front of me, red brakes snapping off as we each accept we can pull the handbrake, take our feet off the pedals. We're not going anywhere. Did they all leave earlier than they needed to like me in case of accident? There's no movement up ahead, this laptop on my knee squashed against steering wheel, a podcast turned off so

I can look and think and hear. And the sky turns pinker and lighter and more striped and the lights of the road go off. It will ruin someone's morning, someone's day, someone's year, perhaps someone's life. It won't touch others at all. Or be a minor annoyance. A call into the office, a child on the way to school waylaid but forgiven. And motorbikes slip between us, they'll know first, they'll see – is it a breakdown, a smash, something terrible. Will we soon hear the roar of sirens? Are there other writers in other cars, laptops open against the steering wheel, engine in park, documenting this halt on the highway? To my right a van, *Specialists in Air Conditioning* which I am against categorically. My children are always putting the car aircon on. I am always turning it off. Ahead of me a number plate JYG. The jig is up. Ahead of the aircon van a Vauxhall Corsa LVR. My lover is not here. And the sky lightens, the pinks fade into dirty bruises against baby blue, the curve of trees and grasses to my right are unnaturally still, no breeze, a silence to them against the noise of road, the cars on the other side passing, the passengers and drivers already rubbernecking, already know what's happened. Movement

TRUTH

When you say you're *sitting in your truth* is it a throne made of gold, diamonds stolen, raised on a plinth so you can see? Is it a camel, seat uncomfortable, weaving its way across desert? Is it a bathtub hot with grimy water, soap lost, toes poking? What does it look like, this *truth* of yours that you bring out as an excuse to tell me something unnecessary. Where were you sitting before that you have to point out the shift in position, is everything else a lie? *I'm sitting in my lie* doesn't have the same ring to it does it, it sounds too honest. And why sit? Why not stand or go the whole hog and lie in your truth like a lover in silk sheets or a pig in shit, writhing. Why not enjoy it. Because Sitting In Your Truth sounds so posed, so oversharing, such a lazy interpretation of growth. *Babe, I need to tell you my truth.* Do you though? Why is that? Who will it serve? Which one of us will be made to feel better? And since when did truth become so possessive? When we offer unsolicited the swirling mess in our heads it's like reporting on a private thunderstorm minute by minute, an ego that says this downpour is important. I've had a Big Thought. It's about you. I'm going to tell it. I heard someone quote Jane Fonda the other day, she said, *No is a complete sentence,* and I love that. It nails half of what I'm trying to say. *Do you want to come to this party. No. Do you like me being here? No. Is this relationship working out for you? No.* There's no need for a lecture, earnest eyes, the seeking of justification. There's no need for the big I Am. You're allowed to be annoying. The other half is this. Because when you've said no, or walked away without saying anything, or kept your Important Thoughts to yourself what you're left with is the uncomfortable feelings, the ones you wanted to fling on my table like a dead cat, the truth that you wanted to make your problem mine. The throne is too hard, the camel makes you sick, the water's gone cold and murky. The truth is that you're the same as me and feelings are uncomfortable and your shit is yours and No is a complete sentence.

LIES

So yesterday's post threw up all kinds of conversations one of which was with a Pure O person who said that for them, truth was a medical matter, they had an obsession with it, and had been through a phase when if they weren't telling everything in their head then they were lying. Truth, lies and shame were so enmeshed that to not speak each thought was unbearable. They leaned on the word *confess* – that's what it was for them, the need to confess everything. 100% honesty meant spilling their guts, a position that seeped into the idea of respect, clouding it. This is the dead cat as gift. What they thought was doing the right thing turned out to be a corpse for the other person. For a time they were in relationship with someone who said, *Tell me everything,* and this open-door policy brought relief for a while though it didn't solve the bigger problem. Those dead cats on the kitchen table piled up, the source of intrusive thoughts is a bottomless pit, there will always be more. And the relief they experienced in not being shamed for all their weirdness did nothing to pull the enmeshment of truth, lies and shame apart. What interests me is this line – *if I don't tell you what I'm thinking, I'm lying.* Because we all – can I speak for everyone?! – I, anyway, have a version of this though I'm not Pure O or OCD or on the A-Typical spectrum. Say I'm convinced you hate me, or you've pissed me off but I still have to interact with you. Say my C-PTSD tells me if I don't sort this out, I'm dead. What do I do with these thoughts that are shouting one thing while my face and mouth are saying another. Am I lying? Or am I dealing with it? My therapist calls it *adopting an air of pleasantness* when I have to be in a situation that isn't wholly where I want to be, and this line is where I've come to rest. I'm obsessed with honesty, too. I can't bear to write something I don't mean; say something I don't believe yet the world continues to behave according to itself and I must be in it. I've come to understand that these intrusive thoughts are everything to do with me and nothing to do with you. My Pure O friend is unpicking the enmeshment as I pick apart the baselines in my own maddened head. The dead cat is my problem, not yours.

FAIRY TALE

Do you remember that room with the fairy sprite who wrote at the table with the candle and quill pen and the pages that flew out the window? And the Angel so huge we could only see its feet, in its arms a baby, and the Green Woman with her arm round the girl in jeans called Rosie who pointed and said *you*, and the Griffin with blue blood dripping from its beak click-clacking, its tail slap-slapping on the steps? How they were gathered in that sunken room that was lowered from the rest of a house beige in its unlovedness, but this room was filled, it had a chaise longue, it had a huge ornate door that was open a bit, not much, enough to show occasionally a view of open road. I went there yesterday to see how they were doing and the door was open, they'd left the room, they had set off. They were heading away, happy, this band of friends, these parts of me collected, they said, *Come on, let's go*. The fairy sprite with her table and pen and candle floating touched her toes to the shoulder of the Green Woman. Rosie straddled the back of the Griffin. The Angel, big feet plodding, walked beside. The sun was shining, it was light and full of beginnings. The road led straight on, not a bend or turn, into the distance. Seeing it reminded me of a book

I was obsessed with when I was little that I've searched for ever since and never found. It was pictures, perhaps there was writing but I remember this: a child in the foreground facing away standing at the beginning of a long straight brick avenue, perhaps there were trees, perhaps there were houses, perhaps it even became a railway but it was straight and it narrowed as perspective dictates. The child stood at the mouth, small to the big path. And as it walked, I turned the pages. Then something happened with size. Instead of the child remaining small and houses and trees growing larger as they were neared, the landscape and road itself remained the exact diminishing size of the first page so that it was the child who grew as it travelled the landscape. By the end the child was huge, a giant on a tiny road with tiny houses and trees. It fascinated me. I turned the pages back and forth trying to work out what was going on. And so we set off. And we shall see.

THE DINING ROOM

Blue walls. I know we've been here before but I need more time. In the corner, floor-to-ceiling shelves and on the highest a square of revolving blue plastic translucent panels that I wanted to touch and wasn't allowed to, they must have been an architectural prototype for some larger design, a present to my mother or perhaps she made them, I wanted to take them down from that high shelf and revolve them on their wires. White rose cornicing. Inveraray Castle at opposing ends, one near, the castle in its detail, one far, how it sat with the hills and loch, an ancient dominance. A thin door to the kitchen always open, and on either side running the length of the wall a fantastic set of built-in white cupboards, a gap between upper and lower that was a shelf, inset and lit and filled with magazines. Above, the glasses we never used, below storage of records and family albums. The record player in the far corner. Copies of the *Architect's Journal* and *Private Eye* piled on every surface, not just the long running shelf, but the low, square, glass coffee table that had lozenge metal loops for legs and was placed between Conran chairs. There the magazines stacked and leaned and toppled onto the long-haired white Habitat rug while on the huge, round dining room table they elbowed for space amongst drawings because this was my mother's domain, this dining room, it wasn't where we ate, and the *Architect's Journal* and *Private Eye* were her career and her politics. The circular dining room table, a silver band running its rim was surrounded by Chippendale chairs and never clear of her work, the piles of things to be done. This is where she was late into the night. This is where her typewriter, so cumbersome it had its own trolley, was wheeled beside her. Or beside me in the daylight hours when she was at her office and I was home from school and had this room to myself; me and my cat and the Duke of Argyll in his wig staring from between vast sash windows heavy with London grime. A stationary island on wheels brilliant with compartments designed by someone who liked pockets and what to put in them, a place for every item imaginable, a shelf for clean paper, a pen holder, drawers that swung from a central axis. Ideal for me and my need to be useful, play secretary, type strict letters, feel worn out by the task. This was the room in which my mother cried at night, she must have, all mothers do and I was drawn to it. There were photographs everywhere, propped on the shining sideboard that had probably come from my father, us in our growing-up phases, a photo cube that I turned over and over. Here I sang along with Sting about the bomb and felt impotent at the window, here I worked on dance routines to ABBA and studied the The Vapours album cover, looking for the people. I kept returning to this room of straight-backed brown sofa and gas fire, Habitat rug and Conran chairs, the magazines falling over. I keep returning to this room of my mother.

BIRTHDAY PARTIES

Note the arms crossed, the hunch of shoulders, a dress she didn't want to wear. The picture is too blurred to give detail to her expression, but I remember. I hope my sister doesn't mind me posting this, I shall ask her when it isn't four in the morning, but her birthday parties were worse than mine – she had more of them, our mother learnt by the time it was my turn that it wasn't worth the horror – and then I found this photograph. Note the tilt of our mother's hand and chin, her arm tense, I can hear her exactly, *Whoa, whoa now just sit we're going to play I need you to listen.* A Very Organised Fun. And there's more. Because according to our mother's politics we went to the local state primary school, a principle I applaud as a voting adult but which meant none of that to us aged five and nine. At the local state primary we were the only ones who lived in a house, everyone else lived in the flats across the road which meant birthday parties were *Why do you live in a museum?* And neither of us had an answer to that. And we didn't really have any friends, maybe the odd one, but not enough for pass the parcel so our mother would insist the whole class came including the ones who hated us. Also, god love our mother, but she wasn't fun. She had other skills; she could bake bread with a hole in it and she filled me with feminist zeal but parties weren't her thing. She wanted them done with, they panicked her, she invented *hunt the banana* which should have been funny and noticed inappropriate and renamed and wasn't. Also, given that we lived in what looked like a museum, why was the prize a piece of old fruit which it often was for pass the parcel too. Oh god, the thundering feet, the screams of laughter, the doors opened that shouldn't have been, the bedrooms looked in, tongues stuck out and fingers up, our secrets trampled, the shame of being seen. Note the girl in the dungaree skirt making a run for it, the boy in the jumper dreaming of his train set. When my children were small I imagined for a minute that I had somehow to do the same, make some arbitrary stab at popularity, a normality that we didn't agree on. And then I remembered how no one enjoys them, how stress seeps up from youngest to eldest and down again. How all children want is to feel loved.

ARISTOCRACY AS CULT

Who knew this would be so hard to write. The aristocracy as cult. And I feel the wrath bearing down on me. I remember when a review in *The Daily Mail* came out of my first novel, the one that takes that class to task, that rolls it over and shows the soft underbelly of poverty emotional, all the wealth and high standing sent skittering across the floor like dropped pearls. I sat on the edge of the bed shaking, feeling sick, my head closing in. Do Not Speak. That is the first and last tenet. Do not show the cracks, the humanness, the sorrow, and never apologise and never explain. I faced a choice on the brink of publication to pull it and remain inside or publish and be cast out. The absurdity struck me even then, this novel that revealed nothing that wasn't already known, that chose to highlight the feelings of people. I knew I was breaking the rules and did it on purpose, those rules being the reason for all those people's sufferings. Those rules being cruel. I consciously refused any longer to collude. It set me free. A writer first, a mother second and all those other identities I was born to, could jostle for third, fourth, fifth. I no longer belonged. But the cult of it, aristocracy as a thing to believe in, the rules and regulations, *we do not behave like that.* It makes me wild; it makes me furious and yet wait, *Try to see it as a religion,* said a friend of mine as I raged. *It's their faith.* I've never been good with doctrines, but I'll give it a go. Imagine: This is how the world works and these are the facts. Here is the map, hereditary titles as signposts to show you the way. *Burkes Peerage* as bible. You can point to your place. Your elders will teach you how to pray. There are stories as lessons, a version of history on which to build your understanding, there are cautionary tales and excuses. In this church of complex rhythms, a mystery to the outside eye, there are promises to keep you safe. Do not disturb the order of things, don't question why, don't you know monarchy is king and god ordained it and when we bow all things are in their rightful place. Don't shatter the edifice with evidence of pain, proof of a thing not working, you will hurt more than this conversation, you will ruin lives. There is more at stake than you. Buck up. Brave face it. Do not bring shame upon us. But no. Because that's the biggest lie of all, that today's sacrifice is tomorrow's greater good and all cults rely on it. *I have your best interests at heart* but you don't, aristocracy as religion, aristocracy as cult. You care only about upholding the existence of yourself. You are the castle wall we die on.

LIGHTNING STRIKE

But it's not black, it's as if the most delicate of tip of giant fingernail has lifted it ground to sky like a child picking bark off a stick. Stripped as if the giant child has taken one long run at it and is pleased with how it forked. Or like the slap of a snake tongue imprinted. Or a toasting prong waiting for dumplings around a family campfire. But it wasn't these things it was an explosion in the night, Andy says I gripped his hand, I don't remember but in the morning when I walked the drive in a hurry to feed the cat who won't come in anymore for fear of her sisters who beat her, the road was scattered with giant pieces of tree – see the strip hanging that never made it to the ground, that must have flown in explosion as the other pieces flew but this got caught and it hangs, testament to something sudden. Yesterday morning I didn't see this rip up the trunk like a child banging its stick on a walk. I only saw the road scattered with great hunks of bark. My head was filled with other things. I had my eyes on my feet and my day and how I had to get a move on. But that night there'd been thunder and there'd been lightning and a storm across the valley that we look upon, high up in our forest, our house hugged by woodland. A shattering in the night that Andy said felt right over our heads and turned out was a hit, direct and lengthways upon this oak who waves at me as I come home each day and night and afternoon. It will dampen, turn musty brown and green, this surface wound that looks so simple yet the hunks that fell on the pot-holed drive were huge and messy and broken. And yesterday a funeral. I stopped on the last bit of road to look how I couldn't look before at the strip torn off in sudden lightning strike, a lit moment that changed everything.

MOTHERING

What kind of mother am I? The over-the-top kind that never misses an opportunity to say, *I love you.* Any excuse to show feeling because it's not obvious to a child, the beating heart of child-rearing; they can miss it. A young person brought a sorrow to me recently, they said, *Why don't they care?* I said, *They do; they don't know how to show it.* Earlier this year I was sent a package that expressed my father's love in a folder of addresses I'd forgotten, a writing down of every mountain shack and beach house I'd lived in all over the world, and it spoke of his care in a way that I hadn't comprehended at the time. Until I held those pieces of paper in my hand, the evidence, his handwriting, scraps torn off the back of envelopes, a postbox number written hurriedly, I imagined the telephone pinned between shoulder and ear, I hadn't known he'd even noticed that I'd gone. And yesterday the same thing happened for my mother. A cousin was going through an ancient box and wrote to me, an email *Just found this!* A report of a conversation between our mothers, detailing a moment I had disappeared in India, there'd been an earthquake, I hadn't been in touch, my mother's *sleepless nights, uncontrollable fears.* Who knew? Not me who was high kicking it around the Western Ghats oblivious, or on a motorbike struggling with wet ropes in the rain. Who never heard her say, *I'm frightened*. I didn't phone home for a year. Imagine. The torment. And now I don't have to because I'm in her shoes, my son is two and a half thousand miles east of here in a school used to war where bombs are falling from Azerbaijan onto Nagorno-Karabakh. And although he's safe in a school with a bunker where three years ago pupils upped sticks for Yerevan to learn in real time the politics of war, and although I tell him every time we speak, *I love you*, I still want to wrap my arms around him and can't and this is what my mother felt and couldn't, or even send a text or funny video or hear my voice in messages sent last week. I didn't know her heart had bled. I'll go and see her. Apologise.

MORNING

I've entered the tired stage, the no-sleep section of the year where I rise at four and go to bed at six, it being the only way to get in the rest needed, my body waking up earlier and earlier so that last year, by the time summer came, I was boiling the kettle at three and sleeping an hour before midday with the effect on my system that I was having two days in one. I don't know when this habit began but since I discovered these magic hours, I can't resist them. I had a breakthrough yesterday. One of those lightbulb moments. *Move chapter seven to the start.* I cut. I pasted. And pow, it was as if the engine of the story came to life. It thrilled me for the rest of the day. I kept returning to it, feeling the rush like fifteen coffees at once and that's what you have to do sometimes, start where the juice is happening and radiate out from there. Maybe the shape of this story is a star. The reshuffle means all sorts of simplifications to the now proceeding chapters, a few technical time leaps, a three-part division of the first act. It fills me with the spice I live for, the reason I get up willingly while all the world is sleeping. The house is quiet, the cats wait in the kitchen for their breakfast. I pulled the winter duvet on last night, another brief waking, cold for the first time since April. My gold-sequinned Dior jacket that I found in a junk shop in the village hangs off the side of the rocking chair. *No one would buy it*; the woman told me. *They said they wouldn't know how to wear it.* My green flight suit on a coat hanger is hooked on a curtain wire strung across the wardrobe mouth, there's a picture of me on the narrow dividing wall aged six in France looking dark under the eyes, wearing my favourite straw hat. In the fireplace, shelves which replace hearth are lined with heels that I don't wear anymore since the pandemic reminded us all that they were uncomfortable. A painting of Edna the donkey done by my RA godmother hangs above them, beside it, a photo of the northern lights over Svalbard, below that a framed poem by my children reminding me not to treat them as twins even though they are. They decorated it with handprints identical. A gold woven sofa with clothes slung on the arm. A black and white image from my pagan wedding, a child in a tiger suit talking to cows. The shutters of the window open onto a blackness, a world still sleeping and I must make my next cup of coffee and get on.

SVALBARD

Once upon a time I went to Svalbard. I had to see the northern lights. My children were small. I left them with their father and took a flight, large and noisy, and then another, small and rickety to Longyearbyen, arriving late, in the dark, getting into the car of a man who only once he'd shut the door and driven off into the icy white, did I wonder if he was a taxi driver or just some random Norwegian loitering for women on their own. Interruption: as I finished that sentence a spider lowered itself from the ceiling, landed clumsily on my dressing gown and panic scuttled into the folds of duvet as I panic threw my laptop off my legs and shooed and scuttled in my own clumsy way, away in the other direction. What is going on today? I feel low. I'm thinking of Svalbard and why I went there and what I want today that I do not have. I went to feel something greater than connection to everyday failures, to be placed before wonder, to shut up my complaining. On the first night I walked off into the dark to get away from the hotel glare and tipped my head into the night and felt the grand emptiness, the deep velvet ghost of that place so vast and silent. The hotel receptionist told me later that polar bears are out there, I was a fool, I could have been eaten. But the romance didn't leave me, the North Pole, a nothing like the nowhere land of life beyond this, and when the mind cannot see where land ends and sky begins it expands. The world seed bank is there, a life craft from every plant on earth in case of apocalypse. There, four hundred nationalities work side by side on that archipelago linked by crystals that are melting. I rode a Ski-Doo across the frozen sea, waves stopped in their roaring, and saw the sailboat frozen in ice where a renegade Dane spends winter. Our heavily padded guide said, *If you fall, don't move, you can get lost here.* It was impossible to tell if the trail was one foot wide or a thousand. I heard stories of abandoned Russian towns and imagined brutal concrete and the echo of footsteps, a lone grandmother hunched in headscarf, a carrier bag, a face at a window without glass. I ate reindeer steaks. I didn't see the northern lights. I was sad and disappointed and vowed to go back. I want to lie on snow wrapped in goose feather down and witness the wonder. I want to understand what lights them up as I understand what lights me, the little wants and big wishes that on some days don't come no matter how far I go, what distance I travel. I am feeling low.

BLOCKED

Do you remember the fairy story? My parts and allies; the child Rosie in her jeans, the Green Woman, her hand on Rosie's shoulder, the Griffin with its tail, the fairy sprite writing, her table and candle and quill flying beside her, the Angel with its giant feet, the baby in its arms? They were off on the long straight road, trees in the distance. I joined them on a horse – Interruption – another giant spider came hurtling across the floor towards my chair. It's disappeared under a footstool. Jeez. Where was I? My parts and allies and I on the road, happy. The next time I saw them they'd set off at a gallop, the Green Woman on my horse, hurtling into the future. For days all I could see was the dust raised by them in the far, far distance. I had a low day when I thought of Svalbard and ranted on the phone to Andy that something was blocking me, it had to be because I was doing everything I could to succeed. He asked what *succeed* means to me, that old chestnut, but I was ready. *It means being allowed to go out and play,* and by that I meant in my favourite playground of books and writing with my books and writing friends. Here's the important bit – *being allowed.* I didn't notice it at the time. I was too angry. I said, *Maybe I'm cursed after all?* and memories of the charlatan shaman came to mind, *You will be cursed for a thousand years,* and it felt as if my parts and allies had galloped off into the future to find help. Andy said, *You have a blind spot,* and I raged at him, *Well how the fuck do you see one of those?* We're coming to the point. Because then something strange happened. I saw in my mind's eye a blood clot, huge and ugly taking up the hallway of the tall, cold house in London. Its sac of a body, across dropped and rising space of stairwells from kitchen to front door blocked everything. Its eye sockets are empty. Its ears are stuck on for show. It has a mouth into which it shovels food with tiny hands, always eating, and it says, *No, no, no, you will not be happy.* I see a miniature me, a tiny adult kneeling before it saying, *Please?* Asking permission. *No, no, no,* it says, stuffing its tiny mouth. It smells. I find I can stand up and walk around it through walls and dropped and rising space. It cannot see or hear me. It doesn't know I exist. *No, no, no,* it says as I pass by, out into the sunshine of the garden, with my friends, to play.

THE UNIVERSE IN MOTION

I've been hearing sounds from the universe. And bizarrely, as I sit down to write, I hear them again. I know it because of this: I was lying on the sofa one day listening to an exquisite celestial music flooding my head when I realised it was coming from outside. Not outside in the garden or drifting up from the valley, its source, and of this I was immediately sure, was a distance so vast, a space so deep, that it was impossible it could reach my tiny human ears yet there it was, reaching, as clear and as loud as if I'd switched on the radio. All right. I get it. My son in Armenia will at this point be preparing to take the piss. Go ahead, my boy. I'm used to it. I've told this story before and no one ever believes me. *What were you smoking?* people have said, laughing. Think what you like because here's what happened next. The sound was of wavering multiple chords like overtone chanting, but wider, colder, it described a source particular and a provenance immense on which I could only focus intently. It went on for ages. The next day I was listening to the actual radio when a man came on reporting he'd recorded the rings of Saturn. And there it was. The exact same sawing drift of thin, wide lines born of a scale unimaginable, a scraping that had filled my head, a wavering of tones across a central constant like the balance of a tightrope walker, leaning this way, compensating that, going on forever in darkness and chill. Lately, in conversations with people whose lives have gone through vast and rolling changes I've heard another sound as they've been speaking, this one a background noise of planets as if mechanisms too ancient for these sentences have taken vast and rolling next positions. I hear the rumbling, cold and constant, the cogs and clanks that describe that place and our small world within it, the epic motion that as you wake from sleep, turn on the light, stretch out your feet, describes you.

THAT NOSE

As the cat washes herself on the counter her shadow moves in such a way that I think another spider is come hurtling towards me. This house of many movements in the corner of my eye. Invariably in daylight I see a figure walk past the window outside. A repetitive spirit, an imprint on my mind, who knows, but I always see it, I always think the postman's here. And I notice also, having done this before, that I describe rooms left to right, as if recapitulating the past with words as we used to do with breath in the pagan commune days. To my left, the draining board of pan upside down, wooden spoons washed up, the taps reflect the light and above them a dark lintel, *Enlightenment At The Kitchen Sink* carved into it. I had it made for all the shamans who sat about telling us how to live while we did the washing up. There are two ginkgo leaves suspended in a glass hexagon that my friend with the magic hands made for me. She knows my love of that tree. I'm going to go on a ginkgo biloba planting spree. If anyone asks, that's what I want for my birthday. There are cactuses on the windowsill, the result of a spate of cactus giving presents; in the space of a week, I received six. I wondered what it said about me. Hanging at the other end is a wooden sign on which I've written in pink marker *have you locked the dog in the car again* because I often did, poor Samson, in my hurry of shopping and children, a car door kicked shut, his forgiving face unseen, a moment much later on, *has anyone seen the dog?* There is a cork board of hexagons, that shape again, only as I write I notice the echo, on which Post-it notes remind me of things I want to say. One says *S.A.D.* Another, *make a fool of me.* There is a sketch by Sophie done while we were all together here, a montage missing only her; I've lodged the origami dragon she made to the top of the collected images so that she is represented, my borrowed daughter who we have embraced. There is a napkin on which she wrote *WILL HOOVER DON'T WORRY xx* left amongst a mess I have forgotten, a teenage note that made me laugh. Below the cork board, a basket of things where keys, coins, pens collect like sticks in a river, the eddies of this kitchen swirl things into it, a piece of gold leather cut off from my boot, some hand cream, a clip with a mouse on it, a blue glass dropper of face elixir for faces growing old. And there is Samson again, a sketch done by an artist at a literary festival who sat behind us and presented it to me when the show was over. My boy, the way his head rests between his paws, the way his haunches round. It will be a year soon since he died. The curve of his shoulders. That nose.

MY DAY

I rode my horse, the midges got to him, we cantered through woods, my friend and I, we spoke about Armenia, was my son safe. Her husband heading north to Georgia knew things ordinary people didn't, she said she'd call him. A dash home to change and out the door again to catch a train to London, my mobile wouldn't charge, *water detected,* it must have been from slinging a bucket at Tommy's undercarriage, he hadn't liked it much and neither had my phone. One hand holding it to air con while the other steered. At traffic lights, I tried again, relief, it charged, I showed my ticket at the station and missed the train. At Waterloo I took the underground to High Street Ken, a message popped up as we popped up from London's tunnels, *I hear your son is in Armenia, pls call.* Immediate worry. The line kept dropping out. He said caution was the better part of valour. He said, *Send a pin drop; I can pick him up.* James Bond-style I saw my son being slung on the back of a motorbike and driven to safety. I ran for my godmother's, burst into her shop and asked in somewhat hysterical style if I could use the office for a zoom call, oh, and hello. I spent twenty minutes listening to the school assess the danger while asking on the parental back channel, *What do we think?* So hard to get a handle on danger when it's two and a half thousand miles away. Refugees are pouring out of Nagorno-Karabakh. The founder of the school was arrested at the border. I messaged James Bond on his motorbike, *I think he's safe.* Tea with my godmother, an hour's gossip. A taxi to Marylebone and coconut curry in *Daylesford* amongst thin women fretting over broth. I walked up the street to Daunts, my brilliant cousin, her book filled the window, I waited for her to appear like *Mr Ben* out of a cupboard in glorious green dress ready to launch herself into her book launch, which she did with verve, a superb writer, she taught me how to write. Her best friend from Paris in white, floor-length frills told me a story of a woman who bought a cellar and drilled into the rock to make bedrooms and took over the street with her dinner parties because there was no room for a table inside. We swapped numbers. I hurried off to find a taxi and missed the train again and sat for half an hour in the evening rush of Waterloo trying to remember the faces. The man who pushed the pram with the bag in it but no baby, the gait of a walk hamstrung with cerebral palsy. The red velvet bow tie on his way to the theatre. The woman in black leather shorts with elasticated waist to whom in my mind I said, *No.* The waist-length blonde peroxide with the silver butterfly clip, her black tights on thin legs, the young station master in flimsy blue tabard who arrived at his desk after I had sat down with sandwich and bottle of water, both of us aware I'd taken position in an area marked out for those needing assistance, but there was no one else there, and I was in my gold jacket, and over fifty, and I could see he didn't dare, or couldn't care, or was kind.

PERFORMANCE

How to write about Marina Abramović? How to write about Andrew Scott and what he pulls off in *Vanya* and I'm not just talking about his top. Did you know he plays all parts? I'll say that again. He plays *all of the parts*. From the moment he walks on stage and flicks the lights, gets a laugh, gets us engaged and on his side and begins to speak, a conversation between Maureen and Michael and we're in, we accept. A slight change of voice, character motifs to make the switch easier; Helena with her necklace, Ivan with his sunglasses, Crater with his face a bit screwed up. Ninety minutes of one man and a family in the countryside on a stage with his props, the ball Michael bounces, the scarf Sonia twists, the Belfast vowels for Alexander, Elizabeth who hardly speaks at all, the dog who appears very late in the action to whom he says, *Where have you been* and gets a laugh because where have any of them been but in our mind's eye and his, this performer who treats us to the impossible. He has sex. Twice. He walks in on himself. He held us in his two hands as if he had hands of eight. And we believed him. And Abramović? The Royal Academy has become her playground till January next year and if you are passing through London or near enough to take a sharp turn, take it. There are naked people appearing in doorways and I noticed how the men walked between them, the women walked around. There is a room that invites you to take off your shoes, put down your bags, stand in rocks, sit on copper, lie with your head in a scoop of stone. There is a skeleton on a breathing woman, she blinks, the people watch. And there is Marina Abramović everywhere in luminous still meditation of thought and practice, the slow washing in a shower, the horse on which she celebrates her father, the flag she holds, the bones that pile, the waves that crash at her face, how her hair drops through the platform under blue sky, how she levitates in the kitchen and carries the milk, her screaming and slapping and the hours she spent staring, there is the table of things when she became object. Performance. Each according to its own, their bodies put through expression, these artists who give or they will die.

PJ HARVEY AND THE DAME
EDNA EXPERIENCE

Not all in one night, you understand, and not on stage together. Two more different acts would be hard to find. I hovered over that word, *acts*, as if it suits one not the other, as if one is true and the other false, an *act* rather than the real thing, but that's not fair, is it, on either of them. Polly Harvey, sylph, genius, a voice of the West Country with fairy dust and thorns written into her twisting hands, her arms that floated shadows on the wall is the real thing; a human who like Abramović and Scott of last week's shows, will do or die. At the Round House, standing in the pit of crowds where trains used to make turning circles, we leaned against the rails that kept the sound engineer safe and were accosted by our neighbour obsessed with telling us how much she loved our energy. This as PJ Harvey gave it the full angelic savagery on stage. Her voice! Her voice, and the crowd devoted raised their hands in glory. Last night I stood two bodies from the rails of the Royal Vauxhall Tavern, squeezed in as a latecomer to the raised platform at the back, a sea of men, two friends and me and the lights went down as we stood up to see. Silver, glitter, purple wig of curls, pink glasses, lipstick, rude, the filth! Glorious, she talked and danced and made us laugh and gasp and sing along and pushed the bounds of every conceivable subject made wicked because she is. An act, yes, and also the real thing. A drag queen who will do or die made famous in her prime, her prime being middle-aged Australian devotion to that other Dame Edna who never faded, who died in her dress and wig and glasses, who lives on. The Royal Vauxhall Tavern like a miniature Round House where queer community make turning circles, that holy place, the heroic centre of London's drag heart, she lifted the curtains to show us fifty years of muck on the velvet hem, and how we recoiled and roared. I bet they'd love each other, PJ Harvey and *The Dame Edna Experience*, both masters, both giving it their all, giving us everything they've got. What it is to reveal yourself like that, be so close to faces staring up, lit by lights that light your sweat and care, what it is to give and give. And we applauded. And they deserved it, every note, every twisting shadow, every sequin that fell upon the stage.

SILVER WOMAN

Remember the blood clot in the hall? I know it's an awful image, it was a blockage, huge and blind, ears stuck on for show, eye sockets empty, a mouth that stuffed food from tiny hands. Monstrous and idiotic and it said, *No, no, no,* as I knelt before it asking to go out. I've been meditating on it and guess what? This happened. From its bulbous bloody centre I saw hands, a body pushing at the membrane that held it jelly-like in form. I saw a figure break through and the blood spill, an oceanic wave of stagnant clotted red hit the walls, washed down the stairs as this figure, slimed and struggling, burst through. She's covered in it, she cannot see or hear yet, the wet sludge sticks to her hair, stretches as she opens her mouth, raises her arms, she is trying to free herself. I'm there with a bucket and cloths, a warm shower, a hose, every day I meditate and we are back at the moment she bursts out almost suffocating, her face obliterated by deep red viscous that I hold a sponge to. My allies and parts have rushed to the scene, we each do our bit to clean, and she keeps emerging slowly, first I saw one blue eye, then silver teeth. I don't know who she is. As we wipe away the blood and pull the membranes from her mouth like a baby born, the airwaves cleared of mucus, she emerges silver every day. And every day as we get to the soft reveal of her face the alarm beside me rings and I am snapped out of that place and returned to the room in which I sit, the candles burning, the yoga blocks beneath my knees. This voyage of discovery never ends does it. Each time I think I've seen them all, another part emerges, she of the silver hair and silver teeth and one blue eye who has lived for generations in a blood clot in the hall blocking me and who knows who else from thinking they can play. The monstrous false-eared, empty-eyed clot is gone and always within the trouble lies another truth fighting to get out.

ROAD RAGE

I wrote this in my sleep *what wanker cuts a cyclist off on a balmy Sunday afternoon in London, their car veering without warning to the left, the cyclist by instinct of survival doing the same* because I was dreaming about this post, not especially this one but this act of waking at four in the morning and writing, and so my dreams are filled with words. It was me who did the cutting off, who wasn't concentrating. I couldn't get over the traffic. I was tired. It had been a long week and these are all excuses for not looking in my mirror in Wandsworth. I saw him too late, the cyclist, only when he swung with the same arc as me, pushed to avoid collision, so vulnerable on his bike, me in metal, but his face didn't look vulnerable as I mouthed *sorry* and when he pulled over and dismounted, I thought he was going to hit me but instead he waved me on with the angriest arm, I didn't know arms could be angry. I thought that was it. I apologised again in my head. Someone leaned on their horn behind me and I thought, *Christ, London's in a mood.* I was glad they weren't shouting at me. The glass towers of Vauxhall rose on either side, the river splashed beyond the buildings, traffic lights changed and I slowed, a black Mazda pulled in front of me and slammed on its break lights. The door opened and a man got out. My window was open. He came straight at me, hands flung wide, furious before I could hear him, *You don't cut people off, you don't cut people off* on repeat, he must have said it three times standing far enough back to stop traffic. But I hadn't. Not him. And that feeling when a car screeches and a door opens violently and a man comes hurtling at an open window. The vulnerability of being seated while a man standing shouts. My face, my body exposed. I think I said, *Oh,* and thought afterwards maybe he was a cyclist vigilante, out to protect two wheels in his four, that the veering episode of ten minutes before was become his bête noire, that he'd followed me, was come for me, that I hadn't been sorry enough. Or he was nuts. Or having a bad day. Or just another wanker like me.

CAT LOVE

Kenny is trying to sit on my computer. She's purring beside me, her little pink nose with its black specks as if she's sniffed the pepper, the run of short fur in a diamond to a ridge at the bridge like two soft oceans meeting, her twitching ears, those eyes that blink. She has one orange ear, one black, the rest of her white but dappled in patches, she has a tortoiseshell tail. She's assumed loaf position, her whiskers so close to my wrist I can feel her breathing. She thinks it's amusing, the way I'm typing carefully so as not to disturb her pose. I woke thinking of Tabitha Twitchit, her photograph is on the windowsill in the bathroom in a silver woven frame. The Queen of my childhood, a silver tabby about whom I laid the silver, I carried her on my shoulders, she slept on my pillow, her purring would put me to sleep. I learnt to cut hearts for her supper, the slime of red and the ventricles rubber, the smell of them short, a musk of lukewarm death. Sometimes she'd have cod instead. Cats settle where I settle, when I came here, we brought Thomas from a newsagent where we'd stopped to buy tobacco and she gave birth soon after to six kittens then moved out to live in the barn. Like Ivy who gave birth to Rosalee Parks, became persona non grata in the kitchen and did the same. The barn is rented to a builder, Ivy's always preferred men. I've made a nest for her under a large stone flowerpot, it has something of the Greek temple to it, I leave food out. The builders are starting to get the hang of her. They're happy they've inherited a cat. She will become their ratter. Kenny has put her paw on the bed table. She rests her head on her leg. I'm told the rhythm and tempo of a cat's purr is the exact tempo used by machines in hospital to promote the healing of tissue. If I can sleep with my head nestled against that beat, I am happy. I feel the waves of her breathing through my bones, her cheek is against the table, that drumbeat of cat rumbling through my blood, healing worry and pain and ancient hurts; she is mending, all the time she is mending.

BOOM-BOOM

I was going to write about Dr. Semmelweis and Mark Rylance and seeing him at the Harold Pinter Theatre with my friend, how we had dinner in J Sheekey and ate tuna tartare and fish pie and her friends joined us who were so clever and impressive I wondered after what I was doing with my life. I was going to say how the play was upsetting and brilliant and I had to leave at the interval to catch a train, how at Waterloo a young man with a spider's web tattoo on his neck and a face that was skewed asked me for money for a hostel to sleep in that night and I refused, not having any coins and also being frightened by his sudden face, the twist of his body, how I felt bad after and went to look for him, found him, gave him a note and was immediately asked by his mate who I refused on the grounds that I'd already done it once and he said, *Yeah but we don't work together.* How I walked away thinking he was somebody's son. I was going to write about all these things until pain broke through a border and caused more pain on the other side, fired weapons, dropped bombs, set off missiles and interrupted two hundred and fifty ravers with a peppering of bullets. They found the bodies yesterday, a field of them, the ones who weren't hurried onto motorbikes and taken, who'd imagined when they set off for that party that they'd be home by now, lying about their bedrooms remembering the pulse of music, not in some foreign place to them but in the afterglow of having danced all night, but no. That's not what happened. The video shows the boom-boom repetitive beat of desert trance, the awnings psychedelic flapping in the sunshine of an early morning, two girls with that up-all-night relaxedness, their bodies moving of their own accord together, elbows bumping, their eyes closed and in the distance something coming. It shows two hundred, more, running across a field, the music stopped, the shouting begun, the boom-boom of gunfire, the bodies that were dancing now panicked and falling, the bodies that had danced all night now lying in a field. I dreamt of a house where they had all gone. It was painted white floorboards and clapperboard walls, it was light and airy and sunshine filled rooms of things they had done, clothes they made, projects they cared about, they walked the corridors busy with the next great thing, how to make the world a better place, a party they planned in the desert.

SHE CROUCHES

She crouches. Surrounded by candles and us, her knees to her chest, her feet flat on the floor, her arms wrapped about her, she crouches. And her teeth are silver sharp. Again and again as she left that fetid, stagnant place, how did she breathe in there, do parts breathe, she pushed off our efforts to wrap and comfort. We hosed the blood away, we warm-showered her with cloths soft and her arms swung and she covered her face as the washed-off slime revealed it, that one blue eye. And when she was clean, we tried to give her blankets. We tried different colours until silver and green seemed to settle on her back as she lowered to the ground, curled in tears and anger, *they are frightened of me*. Because her teeth flashed and she was frightening, sharp as a razor's edge, all of her silver, even beneath the blonde wig she used to emanate something close to human but she wasn't and she tore it off and revealed her silver hair. She isn't. I don't know who she is or where she's from but have I asked that of the others? The Griffin with blue blood dripping whose beak clack-clacks and tail slaps? The Fairy Sprite whose table, quill and candle hover with her? The Angel so large we only ever see its feet? Except yesterday as I sat and watched it crouched with her, huge and gentle, its face came into view and I had to look away. So we sat about her with candles, the blue-eyed silver woman, her razor-sharp teeth, her arms wrapped around legs bent and she cried and shook and was angry and frightened, and as she shivered the Green Woman tried again with a blanket of green and silver and this time, she let it settle. We are all still in the hall of the tall, white house in London, gathered in a superimposition across stairwell and carpet, walls ignored. That house of ghosts and fracture, of stultifying heat and shame and terrible cold, I called it the morgue, where portraits lined the stairs and this silver woman was trapped among so many others. I will watch and she will stand and one day she will speak again and when she does, I'll tell you what she has to say. I hope she leaves that place soon and we can follow her. I'm tired of it. I never want to go back there again.

I WILL DO IT TOMORROW

The sitting room used to be black shot through with silver glitter. I would settle by the fire, wine and spliff, music playing and feel as if I was cocooned in a coal mine or spinning through stars, everyone said it would feel dark but it didn't, it felt as if there were no walls. Some movie people came and shot a film and asked if they could redecorate, they promised to restore it to how it was but I said no, the black depth was over, it was time for a change and about that time I got sober. No more nights staring into the flames repeating scenes in my head of how things ought to be, chasing feelings of love, chasing feeling. But that room I don't sit in either, the sitting room is become a walk-through to my office now that nights are spent eating and going to bed, watching movies from under the duvet. I haven't lit the fire in a long while. There are connections, aren't there, to old habits, the fear and the memory of the slices of pleasure, the deep dive into lost worlds and fantasy, the total shut off from this place where I live now that lighting the fire, turning on lamps, cosying up in my old armchair will bring back. Like music. For the first few years of not drinking anymore I couldn't listen to any, it reminded too strong, it made me want to close the shutters and open a bottle and roll a spliff and settle down to hours of drinking and writing inevitably followed by passing out in front of the TV. That was my poison, those closed-off afternoons, me and my ocean of feelings, plunging depths, building imaginary lives, mine and others, a sense of meaning for a few precious hours, the idea of being someone. The sitting room is white now, the movie people restored order with a lick of their paint. Paintings are hung, the miniature tapestry above the fireplace, Dionysus carved into a piece of found slate in the alcove, the sideboard is propped with photographs, sketches of when we were young, porcelain spoons made by my niece, a nail that fell out of me, another that was pulled, a gold ginkgo biloba leaf that symbolises this growth sustained. I need to write about that room. I need to sit in it and let the memories flood. I will do it tomorrow.

GOD IS IN THE HOUSE

Andy calls these *word paintings*. I like that. I've lit the fire. It burns at my back. I'm crouched on the settle, knees high, I hear its breathing, I'd forgotten how lovely it is. The armchairs face each other across the coffee table, cushions arranged by the last person there, the one to my right has them piled against an arm by my son who'll have sat with his legs sideways dangling, a cat on him purring, all chores released from because who can disturb that. The sofa opposite is as if I have lain longways yesterday. The lamps on either side have odd shades, one dented yellow the other pleated white. It's easy to forget those squat wooden tables on which they sit aren't tables at all but props for a coffin to be placed in a nave and had a body in wood placed upon them, people crying. A pale beam divides the ceiling, on this side to my left hangs a small portrait from The Ellie Heads painted by my friend, she used me as her modal, we met when I'd shaved my hair away. Lower on the wall, drawings of the skeleton of a horse. A long window, broad sill, shutters open to the still dark of early morning, and there is my childhood playhouse, old plastic and red, rescued from London where it would have been thrown away. A table that used to be in the kitchen sits before it, moved there for my son's keyboard and decks, left idle while he's away. Beyond it the cat tower fluffy and ugly, comfortable and cheap. On the far wall, pictures arrange haphazardly above a sideboard of collected things; a close-up photograph of a dragonfly, a screen print by the boy with whom I ran away to India, I think it's the hill of Golgotha but unless he reads this I'll never know. There's a pen and ink drawing of the hallway in France, a painting of my back by the pool, reading, done many years ago, a strange vulture beast sketched by my niece, her porcelain spoons on the polished wood below clink pleasingly when I touch them. There's a charcoal of Samson curled twice, and a distorted by night water body swimming in rainbow costume. It hangs behind the bust of my father, today he wears his tight curled lambswool winter hat and a rosette from the pier at Glastonbury declaring him a winner. There are sketches of my brother and I looking exactly like my children. There are the nails that fell out of me, a photograph of my great aunt, square in tartan, there is a Nick Cave polaroid given me by Andy, it has a black panther in it. And a Pink Floyd vinyl album cover leans at the back, a pig flying over Battersea Power Station, wish you were here. It goes on, this collection, to the wall on my right, the architectural drawings of a brutalist building, a deer and a lion getting married in a wood, a bell jar and the valentines card I made for my Pa when I was five that I thought he'd tossed aside uncaring but discovered years later that he'd kept. The broad wide floor is empty, swept clean, this room of many doors, to hall, garden, office, snug, kitchen and stairs is a gallery of thoughts. And at my back, propped against the dusty black wall, obscured by the wood burner flue, a thin plank of wood declares that God Is In The House.

YES

Yes, said the father when he heard that his daughter was dead, *thank God,* because it was better than the other possible reality, and I heard similar from a friend the terrible year his son died, *Sometimes I think at least he's safe now. I don't have to worry for him anymore.* The impossibility of our children suffering, the incomprehensibility of that thought in our minds, how we cannot live with it, how there are parents who have to, not just in the Middle East but everywhere there is war, starvation, environmental catastrophe, an unsafe home or even the bully at school and off they go to face them. The memory of suffering it evokes in us, of being small and unguarded. The terrific injustice. I didn't want to write about this today but I woke with those words in my head, *Yes, when I heard I was glad.* And I saw his daughter and I felt the tear of being absolved, no longer had to imagine and be sick with fear, and I imagined my own children missing, location unknown, in hostile hands, bombs falling, guns firing, eyes wide, systems shut down, the shattering terror of it and I understood his *yes.* When my children were small one of them disappeared from a playground, I hadn't noticed the second gate, I'd sat by the only one I thought there was, I'd been chatting with a friend and looked up and he was gone, I couldn't see him. We ran about calling in that escalating way that begins with his name in a sing-song voice and ends with asking strangers frantically, but everyone shook their heads. We widened our search to the park, but which way, it was so big; people, grass, trees but no sight of a five-year-old. The heartbeat began, not the visions yet, they were reserved for when I'd found him, when I saw in the distance a stranger holding the hand of a little boy, walking the path toward me, him toddling along quite happily. *I found him on the road,* she said and I didn't stop to take her in, hug her, be so grateful for her kindness and observation, a child alone on the pavement, anyone could have stopped and picked him up. I was too fast holding him and watching the flood of other possible realities fill my brain. They still sicken through my blood even though they didn't happen, I still wonder how I would have lived through them, I walk the corridors of them at night, like the father who cried in relief that death was better.

SHE IS A SILVER DRAGON

To continue with the story. We sit around her with candles, a ring of them, she on the inside, us on the outside, the small flames between us. Still in the hall of the tall, cold house, the dimensions make no sense, the floor reaches invisible across stairwell. She has become quiet as she slumps, the silver green blanket across her back, she is on her left hip, her right shoulder lifted, her forehead to the ground, her arms bent outstretched like an animal injured, and this is what she is as she flickers into silver dragon. And flickers to woman and flickers to silver dragon again, before our eyes. Each scale a silver plate, her teeth sharp, a silver tear drops from a silver eye and she is injured, badly, a wing almost severed, someone had taken an axe to it. Not long ago while out riding my horse he came to an incredible halt from a gallop hurling me onto the pommel, my pubic bone stopped me falling. A week later he leapt and my hand landing hard on the saddle held me in place. Further in the past than that, my right jaw has been hurting, the dentist threatened root canal surgery, I said, *Thanks I'll do it myself,* and have been gargling coconut oil ever since. There's been a pain behind my right shoulder blade, I've imagined it pulsing red like the epicentre of an earthquake you see on TV. And last Friday I saw my Somatic Experiencing woman who works on levels she's gifted for, we've been doing processes simple in appearance but deep in effect, she said, *Has anything happened since last time?* and I told her the story of the silver woman turned dragon, and of the injuries I've accumulated since we last met, all of them on my right side, a meridian voyage from pubic bone to shoulder to jaw to fingers on my right hand. *This part is unfreezing,* she said and we went through the processes again and that night, I couldn't sleep for the pain in my shoulder, as if someone had taken an axe to it. When I was a child, I would see a man coming at me at night with an axe raised when I shut my eyes to sleep. The Green Woman packs the injury with wads of something soft, and The Silver Dragon lets her and we sing. The Fairy Sprite sows with her quill pen, words of comfort into injured wing. Muscles are reattached, sinews mended. My shoulder recovers.

THE WORDS

I wrote something the other day, in the editing I took a word out, and in the comments after that same word was used to describe the essay. It made me think. The habit of overwriting robs the reader of the words they need to describe their reaction. In the editing of a novel that I wrote four years ago, I see that habit taking up valuable narrative space and I've been slashing and burning with all the confidence of four years later. Whole paragraphs cut; sentences disappeared. *Do we need to know this now?* I ask, and *Haven't we already got the point of this?* Because the reader will need words to talk about it. Some have to be left over for them. For every novel I have a folder marked *spare words,* and that's what they are, the ones I couldn't let go of completely, that I keep in case of an emergency that never comes because they know better than me that they are not needed. In the excitement of play there are so many to choose from and I want to use all of them now, this minute. There's the sensation of getting every tin of beans and packet of rice out from the cupboard and throwing the whole lot in the pot as if we won't have to eat tomorrow. Somewhere, too, it demonstrates a lack of faith in the reader. My favourite pieces of literary art are ones where not a word more could be removed, where every syllable is holding up a vital piece of story, like Claire Keegan's *Foster*, when even the title is doing a singular, irreplaceable piece of heavy lifting. And it makes me think also of poets whose words don't crowd the page, Sherman Alexie and A. Jay Adler, two I've been reading here lately, the delicacy of their words chosen to meet the essence they want to tell, because in poems there's nowhere to hide. I sit here now in the silence of predawn, the cat asleep on the table and wait for the words to come, what do they want to say today, how do they want to say it, it's a movement through me that's inexplicable, a force that I live for, and in the editing I see the moments when I got in the way, doubted or wanted to offer every meal at once. And I know when it's over from a feeling, a sensation in my body, stop now.

QUEEN OF THE GYPSIES

I was sent a screenshot and a message on Instagram *is this your ancestor? Did you know she was Queen of the Gypsies?* A portrait by Reynolds, they'd seen it in a show in Portsmouth. The blurb read *Lady Janet Anstruther, formerly Fall (pronounced Faw), her Traveller blood not forgiven by polite society,* or words to that effect, I've summarised. Andy did some digging. He discovered this. They lived at Elie House which her husband, Sir John, had remodelled, extended and generally refurbished to please them both. The village of Balclevie lay unfortunately in their view, Janet ordered it levelled. A woman from the village took umbrage at this and laid a curse on the Anstruther family that Elie House would be lost to them, and that they would have some sort of trouble with the sea. Janet loved to bathe naked, her husband built a tower above a cove in which she could strip out of that pink dress, discard the ribbon tied about her pale neck, throw off those stays and undergarments, climb down amongst rocks to wade out into the freezing waters of Fife and swim amongst the seals. A man servant was tasked with walking the surrounding lanes bell ringing to guard her dignity, warning others to stay away. I read a letter apparently from Reynolds to Walpole, though god knows with the internet it could have been made up, but it reported this: Reynolds went to Elie House as invited to begin this portrait and Lady Anstruther was not there. He observed her likeness in other paintings and was convinced of her great beauty. He took a walk to the beach, hearing that she liked to swim. Edging quietly across the sand beneath the tower he saw a seal bathing on a rock, its body an impossible shade of grey and blue that no artist could capture against the impossible grey-blue of sea and sky. It turned its great seal eyes upon him, he swears that trapped within them were the eyes of that beauty he had come to paint. A siren call of woman turned water beast, and as he watched, it slithered from the rock like mercury poured, and disappeared into freezing water. He heard the bell of the man servant, he was hurried away to the house but caught, before he left, a glimpse of one white arm surfacing and cresting the waves. The Lady's Tower remains as it was built, a folly for a gypsy queen, taunted and rejected for her Traveller blood, who razed a home and brought a curse. I've stood there in the winter wilds of Scotland and watched the seals bathe and dive. Next time I shall wave and call out to her. Let her know also that the house was lost.

LISTENING

I want to talk about nerve endings, the nervous system, mast cells, the language of physical reaction, how our bodies speak to us. My grandmother was a Christian Scientist, my father spoke of how she believed illness was a sign of sin, a sickness in the soul that could and should be prayed away, how she didn't believe in medicine. I often think how this interpretation, such few degrees off at source could land so far off the mark, but that's all it takes, a scope misaligned early on, and you end up shooting yourself when something goes wrong. Because this conversation is tentative, and I'm being careful now, illness as message, sickness as meaning. Because when we get sick the whole story is never the isolated part that's shouting the loudest. I've been working with self-regulation, learning how to regulate my system when it goes into hyperdrive. Sophie asked me yesterday what systems I use and it was a good question because we each learn the methods that suit us, and that we can sustain. Cold baths, inversions and meditation are my three, and I do each in the morning for three minutes. I told her how the cold baths set the dials to zero, how the inversions strengthen my heart, how the meditation is me turning up for myself, checking in, seeing how I am. It doesn't seem like much, does it, yet three minutes in a cold bath can feel like forever and three minutes is all my system can cope with when I enter the land of sitting still before the great Unknown; I'll get into why that is tomorrow. The point is that however small or slight these movements are, they form a practice of alignment which builds a habit of familiarity, and when I'm out in the world and find I'm running, it's these sensations I can reach for to bring me back together, *Hello inside of me, it's okay, I'm here.* I've a friend who became very sick with long Covid and in order to save herself developed her yoga teaching practice into a recovery program which now holds the hands of millions of long Covid sufferers around the world. Her clients return to their doctors showing signs of recovery and their doctors say to my friend, *What is that you're doing? How are you getting these results?* The answer to that is more than one sentence but for the sake of this moment I'll sum it up with *I listen. I let them tell me what they're feeling, and we work with that.* This is the part we can bring to the table when we're sick, the part that can work in collaboration with whichever medicines we like. Our nervous systems are speaking all the time, sending messages, trying to keep us safe. Listen.

MEDITATION

Leaning over an abyss, a blackness into which I would topple, a nothing to swallow me whole. *Close your eyes and breathe* but I felt as if I was falling. At Vipassana I was held to some degree by the form and the room and the others and the person sitting up front, ten days silent when I wrote poems on my pillow, a pencil found beneath the bunk room doormat, a contraband passed on. But then we came home. I remember my husband having no trouble at all with the hour at morning and night, he'd sit, the picture of Buddha without the fat, still and smiling. But I had a tingling through my muscles telling me I was going to vomit any minute if I didn't open my eyes and move. I rang the centre in Hereford, they advised me to try it lying down. It didn't help at all. I felt suicidal. And so I stopped. I didn't sit for many years, I don't remember what got me into it again, I do remember feeling bad about it, being down on myself, thinking I wasn't trying hard enough, I was lazy, a coward, an imposter. *All this spiritual lark and you don't meditate?* I kept it hidden. I remember telling myself that anything could be turned to that frequency; walking, running, doing the washing-up, that even this, writing, is a meditation of sorts, but I didn't believe any of it. In my heart I said I had failed. And then I met my Somatic Experiencing woman who operates on levels I marvel at, who is the finest example of quantum healing, where science meets the Great Unknown, that I have come across. *If childhood authority figures were not safe or not there, meditation will be an impossible task. It will feel dangerous.* And there it was. My exact experience summed up in her careful words. Meditation frightened the hell out of me, it always had, and I'd always blamed myself for not being courageous enough to face it. But being a very courageous person, and now with the knowledge that my body, with all its resistance, wasn't wrong, I tried sitting for one minute with my eyes open. That one minute has become three. I've tried four, it doesn't work, I am frightened again. So, three it is and I sit on my mat and turn up for myself and know that the body keeps the score. It's learning with me that I'm not alone after all because I am there, sitting within the Great Unknown that is filled with stars and points of light like this, my beating heart.

BANK

The child on the roof has their hands in prayer, they face not quite to the front. A chimney cowl and pot, a brass roof, four corners, a slit so narrow it's a wonder coins were that slim. The front of the building, five windows and a large brass door, *BANK* is moulded above the lintel. Yet the sides are like church windows, I imagined them stained glass, while the back is as if it were a birdcage or prison, diamond holes in a pattern, enough to curl your fingers through if you were small. All of it sits on a wooden plinth with steps from the grand entrance to the table where it is beside me this morning, moved from its normal windowsill place because lately when I've visited the land of parts and allies, the fairy story unfolding, I've seen the walls of the tall, cold house in London collapsing like this child's toy. Untwist the child with hands in prayer and you'll see. Turn them anticlockwise, lay them aside. Lift the cowl, take the chimney pot with it, be ready when you dislodge the roof. *CRASH* the clang of the walls falling would thrill and worry me and I would repeat it over and over even though to put it together again was the fiddliest of businesses, I needed six hands and I only had two. Yesterday I showed Sophie and Blake, *What's that?* as I brought it from library to kitchen, and *Why?* because this is what's been happening in the other place. Do you remember where we left off? In the hall of the tall, cold house in London where candles circled the Silver Woman turned Dragon, and a terrible gash to its wing was a wound as if someone had taken an axe to it. We were singing. The Angel in whose arms the baby has lain put out its great hand, the Dragon suddenly small, scampered like a child's toy, melted into the baby and they became one. Onto the shoulder of the Angel it clambered, silver wings spread, silver claws gripping, and the Angel stood, and we rose with It, and the roof dissolved in light. Rosie in her jeans astride the clack-clack Griffin, the Green Woman upon a winged horse, the Fairy Sprite fluttering easily; *So many wings!* I thought yesterday as I watched them rise from the hallway, and the air was pierced bright and the roof came off and the walls fell *CLANG* in flat concordance smack upon the ground and I kept thinking, *What does that remind me of?* and then I remembered. This child's toy my godmother gave me when I was small. She has a shop that is a cornucopia of treasures. It's under siege by developers who cannot understand that they will be destroying a universe. I will write about it tomorrow.

THE LACQUER CHEST

I think of the bell that rings and the floor that creaks and the stairs lined with hats and the tiny upstairs loo where the shelves are crowded with perfume bottles. I think of the writing bureau with chair pushed away as if my godfather has left only moments ago, and the garden table downstairs in the back where we made tea and ate pastries, the low chair, the door pinned with *thank you* and *Merry Christmas!* and *we're loving our* notes from clients who became loyal, who became friends. I think of the yellow walls and worn-out stairs and green, damp yard of pots and wooden wheelbarrow and the hours spent in the basement with porcelain and China and dinner sets, packing and unpacking boxes of plates, the paper wrapping, the fear of breakage, the happiness of that summer. My godmother's shop, which was also my godfather's, and in fact it was him who was named at my christening but it was both who took me on, and now that he's dead long ago I've adopted her for the moniker and she agrees, my godmother's shop is a fairy tale. Not if you have a headache, this antique wonderland is a mass of complication, but if you're straight out of school and in need of a job, if surrounded by thimbles and drawers of spoons and *This is where we keep the snuff boxes* and out come hundreds of every kind, if a Lacquer Chest family is what you need then these months of tucking platters in bubble wrap will make you happy. The stairs wind up and up, become narrower, each room a dedicated haven to linen, silver, pince-nez, glass and glove. If you've seen a period costume drama, you've seen the hankies kept in tissue, the epaulettes stored boxes, the picnic sets and blankets which will be flapped upon a lawn. Elizabeth Bennet will fill these baskets with flowers as she walks in the garden with her father. Anna Karenina will rattle her cup at the samovar as she lowers her eyes to Count Vronsky. Leonard Bast will open an umbrella. It's a world beyond a street, a labyrinth of old, forgotten, gone. Pipes no longer used in heavy armchairs, hats no longer worn to go to work, a beaded cloth draped over milk jug keeps the flies away, but who needs that. And when I go, I go of course to see my godmother sitting in her chair by the till, but also each time I say *Do you mind if I just* and off I go, upstairs or down, it doesn't matter, all is a wonder of lost and found time, a Mr Ben magic beyond the green and gold door, a universe hidden from the street, a bell that rings.

BEASTING

I need you to forgive me says one part to another, the part of me that is plagued with what I've done wrong. The Luna Park episode when Jacobi hustled for an all-rides ticket then refused to go on any and I lost my shit, how he sat on his bed that night looking frightened and it hit me that he had only been being a child, that's what children do, and I had slammed him for it, how that image haunts me. How I never realised Blake was neurodiverse until at twelve it dawned on us, how I wish I'd known the world that spun inside that head, how I imagine loneliness and feel the stab of it. How I shouted when a kitchen chair flipped backwards just as I'd put the supper on the table, how I said, *Get out,* when one of them playing with a resistance band snapped it so hard it made me jump. How I fuck up again and again as a parent, friend, sibling, partner, host, mishandle this life, how this is human, and the part that beasts me for it. I sat before my altar and heard the other part of me say *I need you to forgive me,* because how can we go on with this internal beating, what is the point of it, where does it get us, what does it do, and where will it end? Accountability flips into neurotic self-hate, guilt, a shame indulged in, and do you hear it already creeping into that sentence? The stick is out, and in the hand, even as I write those words, even as I delve and look and bring it onto the table. An aggressive approach to the inherently flawed experience of being human, a zero-tolerance attitude, I don't know where I learnt it, I am frightened, a lonely world spins, let's look.

I DO KNOW WHERE I
LEARNT IT

I've said this before, but I'll say it again because it goes to the heart of the matter. To be human is to be vulnerable. If being vulnerable is too much, being not human is the answer. That was the solution a part of me came up with. We will be not human, and we will be safe. Imagine a parent with its hand over the mouth of a child, keeping it quiet so that invaders won't hear where they're hiding. If the child makes a sound, they're dead. This part of me said don't show fear, don't have feelings, don't give away any sign that we're alive and made of flesh. It's too dangerous. It was a brilliant answer to the problem, and it worked, I stepped outside of myself for a long, long time, and for a long, long time I wasn't really here. I was superhuman, I could do anything, nothing could touch me, I didn't care. But what I didn't realise was this. To be human is to be vulnerable to mistakes, dropping something, hurting someone, getting this life wrong. The part of me with its hand over my mouth says, *No, shh, you're giving us away.* In its beasting, it believes it's protecting me. Have you read *Internal Family Systems* by Richard C Schwartz? This is what I'm talking about. The universal commitment to survive, and the solutions that parts come up, persisting long after the danger has passed. *There's a part of me that* – this is the starting point phrase. There's a part of me that beats me up for things I did years ago and yesterday because those episodes, so human in their everyday flaws, give away my whereabouts. I hurt and I make a sound. To make friends with the part that beasts me, to understand its actions, to tell it that it's done a great job, and it can rest now, to ask it what it wants and what it needs to put the stick down, these are the forward movements of integration. When I wrote that line yesterday, *I don't know where I learnt it* I knew it wasn't true as I read it over, but kept it in because it felt right, and realised the instant I pressed *publish* it was because I would write about this today. We're getting close to the end of *The Recovery Diaries.* We're getting to the heart of the matter.

THE GREAT BLUE YONDER

Some mornings I've no idea what I'm going to write about. A blank sheet. That's what I went to bed with last night and woke up with this morning. Nothing, except the image of a pain body being winched from a basement and who wants to write about that? Not me. The parts and allies floated up into the great blue yonder as the walls of the house fell smack to the ground like a Buster Keaton sketch, and they hover, now, in glorious, funny blue line, they are waving goodbye. *Goodbye?* I think, *But how can that be? They are me.* And I don't like it, but the rules of this game are such, these are not stories to be orchestrated, they are to be watched unfold. That's what I've done since the beginning, since the very first time I found myself in the swimming pool in France where I spent the happiest childish suspended hours balled up, knees to chest, turning with the water and saw turning with me the red, knees to chest sinews of my pain body. I remember, and somewhere in these diaries is the story, how it looked like a filter that hadn't been changed, how it was a William Blake drawing in the detail of muscle and elongated leg, how it had its arms around its knees like me, and I remember the overwhelming feeling of love for what it had done. Since then, we've been through Gremlin to teenager in high-windowed cell, white nothings to the dream of a house attached to mine where absence was described in beige, to a sunken room that began in pitch black and became filled with my parts and allies and a door, ornate, that one day we went through. We've returned to the tall, cold house and found blockage and cleared it and watched blood pour down basement steps and a silver woman emerge. We've seen them all rise. But *goodbye*? And then that damned image I woke with this morning, the pain body winched, more blood dripping, have we not had enough by now? What is the darkness of my mind, the hidden corners from where this must be wrenched? But I know. I've done the work and I've seen. And the rescue goes on. And my parts and allies float into the great blue yonder, and I see them hover in a line, they are waving merrily and laughing.

A LOW-BEAMED COTTAGE
IN THE COUNTRY

In the low-beamed cottage I had a cot, large and wooden, with a side that slid down with a clattering snap. Occasionally I'd figure it out for myself, often I'd climb out anyway over the high bars. This cottage of my father where we'd come at weekends, invade his quiet space with crash of ten feet, ten hands, five voices and my mother, had a rock garden through which a small river was diverted, the sound of water our lullaby, me in my wooden cot drifting off to the sweetness of the stream, and the tinkling of bells on my father's Turkish slippers as he moved across the tiles downstairs. I had my soft toys gathered about me like worries, my teddy, an elephant, I don't remember them all, but I remember the cluster of them. And I remember toddling about, getting out of my cot carrying them. What was I worried about? That cottage was safe, it was warm and snug, there were no interlopers, my father kept a tight ship. There were never unexpected arrivals with suitcases asking for a bed, surprise guests who never left, sharp-nailed nannies giving us baths, strangers on the landing. There was no basement. Perhaps I didn't want to leave. Perhaps they argued in the night as parents do when all children are asleep, or parents think they are. That cot has come back to me, a forgotten bed that I loved remembered, wide and deep, the wooden slats blonde and smooth, the red plastic catch that could be snapped and trap your fingers, the small rectangular mattress and scratchy green blanket. I, the youngest, was the last to use it, placed in my bedroom between single beds that I would grow into. Curtains floral and large-printed in colours of *The Magic Roundabout*, red and orange swirls of the seventies, this is how I remember them, but memories can be wrong, I was there yesterday, and they are gone, replaced with something shiny bright and awful, they must have become threadbare, I miss them. A picture on the wall remains, white plastic frame, electric blue the background to a bowl of fruit, fantastical, large and sparkling, the nest of a dove with a diamond eye. A shelf of Beatrix Potter books, a cupboard with a sliding door, this cottage of few rooms has treasures everywhere. We've spent so long in the tall, cold house in London but now that it's gone, we can come here, to the low-beamed cottage in the countryside, where I was worried-happy, where on Friday nights we'd park the Citroën in the garage, leap to close the pull-down door, run in.

SWING

To the beginning before any of this started, because for each of us there is a time before. I think of that person, who had it all coming; no wonder she was worried, did she know? Or did she sense an atmosphere where it was possible, something terrible, simply because no one was watching? I see toddler me, two-year-old me in my cot in my bedroom in my father's low-beamed cottage surrounded by her soft-toy worries and I cannot take my eyes off her. She's standing up, leaning against the bars, looking at me with those big blues, and she's listening. She has the face of a child who doesn't understand. The duvet on the bed is green like the woman who picks her up and holds her, sits on the edge of the single bed, and cradles her, whispers it's going to be all right, but she's caught by a sound inside her head, and I want to stop time. These are the feelings that haunt me, the sense of knowing, and the powerlessness to stop it. The impending death I paint onto pictures in my present day, my friend calls it *Mrs Armageddon,* her version, the emotional flashbacks that swamp. These are the colours of my C-PTSD, the worry me searching like a radar over water for the possible deaths approaching, the translation into the everybody-hates-me's as a way of staying safe, a habit, a narcissism born early and arrested, the worry me leaning into the bars of her cot. In the garden of the low-beamed cottage was a Mouse House built beside the lake we were told was made of quicksand. A woman had escaped from an asylum and drowned. We must never go near it. This room of brick and tile, a mouse weathervane on the roof, a blue door, metal windows on two sides, the paint is peeling, was where my father wrote his first book. He would take himself away to this quiet spot, a man of ghosts and hauntings who built a life to survive his worry-self, stories to keep us away, who found joy in an order constructed on the page. I'm walking through the garden now, up across the lawn to the small river, along the paths cut through long grass, past the ginkgo biloba tree he planted from a seed brought back from Washington, into the shaded undergrowth where the riverbanks become steeped in roots and a swing let us fly out in a circle shouting, where Alice fell and didn't break her back but we all thought she had. I'm aware that time is doing something strange; I'm swinging from two, to five, to fifty-two and back again; I had two lives, one in a low-beamed cottage and one in a tall, cold house. I'm in the garden amongst the shouts of play and sunshine, the Mouse House sits quietly, the lake is still, there's something for me here. I am searching.

SUMMER

I nto the garden where we played Banana Split, running over the plank bridge and returning by rope singing *one banana two banana* manically until we were spent with it and someone fell into the shallow, happy stream. Into the garden where the sun always shines unless it is Christmas when it snows and we take our toboggans to the top of the hill and fly the Cresta Run from woods to garden, clinging on at the ridge, flattening at the barbed wire, in one heroic effort once, one of us made it to the sitting room, arriving covered in icicles before the fire. But that was winter and we will get to that because this is summer and the meadow waves long and blonde and the bees hang lazily in dizzy warm air and we play Lions In The Jungle on hands and knees in vast fields, setting off from different corners, crawling and roaring and stopping for a scratch, padding through the Savanna of West Sussex until a rustling produces each other, chance meetings in an ocean of long grass. We'd go fishing with our father, the banks of secret rivers thick with brambles to catch trout that we'd release into the pond at home or eat for supper, he taught me how to slice and gut, I could never do the banging on the head. My sister squeezed a pot of yoghurt at my other sister in a game after lunch when we were supposed to be bringing pudding to the long pine table, covering her in white slosh, my father yelling at my mother, telling her to tell us to behave, my sister said she didn't know the lid would come off. The excitement of being there, a precious jewel in a cold London crown, these weekends in the country, the smallness and the comfort, the dead mice under the carpet where the cleaner, in love with the gardener, would sweep them. Napoleon Timlick had jug ears and rode a motorbike, a flat cap and capable hands, his was the woodshed where I loved to sit, its dark order and damp and wood chips, the sawhorse and axe, there was always dry wood for the fire. And in the early years, the ones when I still had my cot, our housekeeper from London was there too, who would make shepherd's pie and chocolate cake with an orange marmalade filling, I see her smiling as I enter from scullery to kitchen, I must be small because she is huge, the bulk of her apron, the curls of her dry set perm, her hands in a bowl, the Aga warm, the red tiles, I can feel the cracks beneath my feet.

AND THEN WE GOT PONIES

And then we got ponies. My father gave me to the farm manager, *Look after her, Mayes*, outside the church, sunshine, the farmyard heavy with sloped roofs and chestnut fencing, puddles and mud, the threshing barn beyond where a boy had died falling into the blades and we were told not to play so of course we did, climbing amongst bales, deadly and the smell of dust. Another barn piled with hay, the blue pickup truck parked in a bay beside barrels where potatoes grew, and in the corner by the church wall, the pump for tractors that my father used to fill up his Porsche, so exciting to have our own petrol. *Mr Mayes to you,* embarrassed I'd used the same phrase, his enormous white curly-haired dog beside him, Bumble, who howl-spoke. We got ponies. These were my weekends now, ride my bike up the lane to Bella, in from the field, muddy and soft, grooming kit, tack room, kissing her mealy nose. Do you know I've begun and deleted this post five times, there are so many memories flooding my brain, a sluice gate raised like the one in the stream that stopped it overflowing and flooding the cottage in winter. Last night I dreamt of the sitting room, green sofa, fireplace stacked with wood, white, long-haired rug like Bumble's coat, but straight. I was stoned out of my mind, there was a woman with me, she had greying permed hair. She'd smoked the spliff I'd been handed ready-made by a young man who'd laughed when I'd said, *What is it?* and I'd had to clarify, *Is it grass, charas?* I'd smoked and given it to this woman who was lying on the floor and now she was crying, her arm raised to her forehead in despair, she was saying, *I don't know who I am.* This is what happens when you open a door, the ghosts come rushing, *me, me* everyone wants to be heard and seen, this need to be recognised and understood doesn't stop at death. This is the rule when this happens: pick up the first image and go from there, they will lead you like a trail of crumbs through all of it. Grooming my pony, Mr Mayes in green quilted coat and flat cap teaching me how to do up the girth, red numnah, the reins between my fingers, riding out, we reach the Common and he flings the lead rope over Bella's neck and takes off; this is how I learnt to ride, get yourself together quickly, no pony wants to fall or be alone.

HER FIRE

Picking apples in the orchard, being sent to the fruit cage, I still can't eat red currants. My mother baking bread, always the hole in it, she couldn't figure it out. Warm from the Aga, still on the cooling rack, butter, and strawberry jam. Jars and jars of her pickle and jelly in the larder. I think she was different here to the architect in London, head in hands, exhausted. Here she baked and gardened, we got her riding again. Jerry and Siri, son, and mother, he enormous and grey, she tiny and Siamese, always meowing. My marble run in the upstairs hallway. Playing tiddlywinks on the sitting-room carpet, scrambling in the hanger where the Gremlins lived. Those woods that dripped in August, the steep rise of them, the cavernous drop to the stream that sprang from a spring we would trace, splashing our way upriver, climbing over fallen trees, inching along logs that had become moss-covered slippery bridges. The sand of the riverbed, the clarity of the water, the stone chalk and grey, pheasants squawking, rabbits hurrying, badger dens, and deer in sudden light. The cuckoo calling in summer. And desperate to pee, my siblings older, faster, I sat down in the current of water to hide that I'd done it already and ran home to pretend that I'd fallen.

My mother washing my jeans in the sink and saying again and again, *What happened?* until my shame was properly explained, I wished she'd stop asking. Supper in the kitchen at the square Formica tables that wobbled on the uneven floor, the chair with horseshoe shape in its seat, the curtains drawn along the long window of many little windows, a tiny sill for each. Lighting the fire, cleaning the candlesticks, turning napkins into bishop's hats for the dinner parties I would miss. My father's margarine decanted into tiny round white pot and put beside his place at one end, my mother would be at the other. Shared friends except if they were Tories like my father, she sat them under the low beam in the dining room so that on rising after lumpfish and venison and wise cracks about war and how Thatcher was the best, they'd smack their stupid heads and leave bleeding. I'd listen from my bed, sometimes the stairs, peering through wooden railings, pyjamas, feet bare, politics exchanged with the gravy and burnt carrots, how he laughed, and she raged, the guests drunk, the candles low, *you can always give up your horse,* a jibe that got her, his money, her fire.

AS LONG AS THE EYE

I think I know who the Green Woman is. When I saw her last week, I told her I'd seen me as a baby in my vast wooden cot and as I spoke, I remembered how the Green Woman had appeared and lifted me out and held me in her arms, and I put two and two together. It's the tempo of them both that gives it away, she in this world where I type, and she in the world where I go. It's the same. I'll never tell her, this ally who moves across worlds with me. It would be awkward. So this time when we met, my healing somatic woman and I, off we went into the strings and tensions of my nervous ends and I was back in the room with me in the cot but this time I lifted me out and took me outside into the garden of the low-beamed cottage where the Angel, huge as always, held out its hands to take small me, and carried me into the field where the ridge in the Cresta Run made our toboggans take off. But this vision was late summer, the air still and warm, the harvest already in. My Somatic Green Healing Woman said, *How do you feel?* and it was odd, I didn't have words, I had sensations which I associate now with fear, anger, confusion but in this somatic-embedded state it was like landing on Mars and not speaking the language. I described a fuzziness, a sensory haze and she said, *You're wandering in the messiness of preverbal trauma,* and although that sounds awful, I loved it, the phrase, because it explained it exactly. I spent the session standing in the field watching the Angel hold small me, the dominate emotion a cloudy, invisible threat, *what is this,* as if I had walked into cobwebs in the dark, so odd in the vision of sunshine. No wonder the amygdala stands up and looks, no wonder I was on guard. Yesterday a friend came to lunch and brought me *What Is It That Will Last?*, the work of Julie Brook recorded in photographs, her collaboration with nature. We talked about how the artist focuses, *why* is answered *because I must* and these fires she builds in water last as long as the sea rises. And these fires I build in words last as long as the eye pauses.

HOW TO SQUARE A CIRCLE

What I can't understand is how bad things can happen while being held by an Angel, because I'm standing in the field watching small me in huge arms and for the first time in this process I'm conflicted; I want to interfere with what I'm seeing, I want to change history. I don't want to grow up, a year to pass, that shadow man to arrive, bad things to happen in a basement, I don't want to be returned to my cot in the low-beamed cottage, I want to stay in those Angel arms forever, the late summer sun shining on a field where in winter we'll toboggan. Yet, of all the myriad magics available, changing the course of history is not one of them. Events happen. And what difference will it make now, in the replay of this block universe where my birth and death and yours and everything in-between is happening all the time and all at once? That these subtle changes are made, I'm held now, not so alone yet still I must go through it, blows my mind; it's a circle I'm finding it very hard to square. Yet Andy and I spoke yesterday of humans, how given self-consciousness, the skill to shake off trauma, still innate in other animals, was lost to us, how we must consciously remember to do it, and how we don't. And these are the differences we make in this work, to go back to the beginning of the universe and do it right this time, not change events but witness them at their right size, and act accordingly, be there for ourselves, shake out the terror and invasion, these are the differences that our bones remember. Yesterday I said it felt like walking through cobwebs in the dark, these sensations I had no names for in the preverbal messiness of the before, and last night I dreamt I was in the kitchen of my father's cottage and my leg was covered in hard bubbles of spider bites. It had orange stripes on its legs, I saw it disappear down a crack in the floor, I ran for a candle, I would pour wax after it, seal up the hole, and this time I could see the trails of its silk everywhere, reaching from the window across low-beamed ceiling, wafting in the breeze from an open window. I climbed the steep stairs to bed. I had sensations everywhere. Winter is coming to that cottage in the country. The windows will be shut, and the curtains drawn. There will be a fireworks party. There will be Christmas.

REMEMBER REMEMBER

The story goes that the fire brigade were called by a neighbour across the fields who saw flames and ever since then they were invited, the firemen, not the neighbour, to the party in the Black Barn that my father threw for estate workers every November 5th. Mr Mayes began building the bonfire in October, huge, it had a door, this fascinated me, imagine living inside it before it was burnt. It was set in the field below the stud farm, lights were strung on the yard doors, this was important, a secret signal would be given. But first, a party. The Black Barn had a rounded roof, was made of wood, a dirt floor, wide-open doors big enough for a tractor to drive in and turn around. Trestle tables were set on two sides, there would be hot, mulled wine, I remember the vats of it steaming, and beer I suppose though it passed me by. There would be sausages which didn't. Freezing cold, winter already set in, was the Christmas tree up outside the cottage yet? I don't remember. But I would see the bonfire grow and the stakes that would flame be stuck in the ground and the fireworks that would whizz bang explode be unloaded from a truck and set about, there was no string to stand back from. The firemen and fire engine, guests in uniform and the rest of us in wellies and anoraks, all the men and women who worked on the estate arriving in pickups and Subarus, the chatter growing louder, the barn growing warmer, the crowd shouting over each other, greetings, quilt jackets and flat caps, children running, weaving through legs, knocking elbows, asking for mince pies and my father, the king, at his happiest, saying, *Time to ring the bell.* It was almost heavier than me, it took two hands, I'd have to swing it low, back bent, ringing with all my small might, clanging the Black Barn to silence so that my father could stand on a crate and thank everyone for coming, for being part of his world, for making it better. And then a fire torch into our hands, my brother and me, and a procession, small flaming leaders for the length of half a country lane and into the field where there were no barriers or safety wardens, where everyone knew to stop while we carried on into the bonfire space and turned to watch, over the heads of the crowd, the lights on the doors to the stud yard for the secret sign. Two flashes of the bulbs, the bonfire door opened, our torches thrown in and up it went, a glorious fire lighting up the November night, our fireworks party, the whizz bang set off, our faces lifted, all of us happy, this version of family complete.

SOME PLACES

I've been feeling sad. These memories, like pheasants flying up as I ride past, have upset me. Those weekends and winter holidays in the country were warm and happy, and even though my father was tense, and my mother harried, they were together; we were all together. It was safe. We lived a double life in this standard of plenty, he had his way, she had hers, Sussex and London, they were more than a car ride apart. My father stayed in his cottage when we left on Sunday nights, he came up vaguely only sometimes to town, a lemon in his pocket, to hunch at the kitchen table. The low-beamed cottage was his home, and those two places were vast in their oceans of difference. The tall, cold house is gone now and since it fell apart, I've been here, wandering the messiness of endless summers, and bright, cold winters. I see the lights go up on the Christmas tree outside beside the well that the vicar used to bless even though it was only my father's bathwater hidden beneath an ancient head and bucket. I see the sitting room through the window, cosy and warm, the brick fireplace stacked with wood, the heavy black iron fire dogs, the secret bread oven, I see the four armchairs, each a loose cover faded colour, yellow, brown, blue, and orange, and the collapsing green sofa on which there was always a cat. I see the round table by the glass doors that had the little balustrade like a balcony for mice. In the corner was the miniature library with tiny window, above which, in my parents' bedroom, was the cupboard that led to a secret room into which I'd crawl, pushing coats aside, my Narnia, waiting for Aslan. I see the wooden head of my eldest sister, braced by a pair of golden lions on the windowsill of the upstairs corridor, downstairs are the other clay ones of us. There we all are, gathered on Christmas Eve writing letters to Santa Clause, a fire built up, our father handing out thin paper and pens. On the settle, its leather torn by scratching cats, I sit knees up, my letter on a book, and write *Dear Santa* and when I'm done my father lightly scrunches it up and holds it on the toasting fork above the flames for the draft to whisk it up the chimney; even if it falls, he'll say it still works. Out come the stockings when we've gone to bed, I imagine my parents surrounded together with boxes of gathered little things, the chocolate coins and walnuts, the tangerines and sugar mice and packs of mini cards, while in my bed I try to stay awake but sleep, listening to the stream falling endlessly through rock. Once I woke as he crept in with my stocking loaded and wrapped in tinsel, I saw my Father Christmas lay it on the end of my bed. But was the spell broken? No. The spell of that place remains even now I am grown, have a home and children of my own. Some places are always Narnia. I wanted to stay there forever, for the end of winter holidays or Sunday nights to never come. But this was Christmas Eve, and in my bed, eyes closed pretending, I heard my father creep out of the door, felt the reassuring weight of Christmas stocking with my toes. Tomorrow we'll pile into their bed, all of us, a mass of tinsel and opening small gifts, my father trying not to spill his tea, my mother crowded by the bodies of us.

OH CHRISTMAS

Christmas Day was a swear word in my father's vocabulary, said any time of year with stamping foot, making us scatter and laugh. Sometimes he'd take his lunch to the garage, eat it staring at the shelf lined with cobwebs and redcurrant jelly, his chair shoved up against the freezer. But actual Christmas Day was one of exacting repetition, everything, always the same. Stockings, our parents' bed crowded, we could make a tinsel mess. Church, running up the lane, ringing the bell, the pull of that scratch rope, the tiny chapel filling with coats and scarves and icy breath, becoming hysterical singing, *Hark the Herald Angels*, I still can't stand between my brother and sister in a pew without losing it. The silver platter being handed along for coins, my father taking it to the altar, his bow that we knew meant precisely nothing; as parish warden he loved to say how he never went to church. Except today. Drinks at our neighbour's house followed, a chore escaped if, and this was more special than presents or lunch, you were chosen by him to go quietly along the stony lane to collect those shiny wrapped parcels from his studio, the secret locked place above a stable block that held treasures, mostly him. The stamp and chill of an outside staircase closed as an afterthought, but thinly. A half glazed green door, the warmth of his small and orderly room, rugs and round table, a little kitchen, kettle and sink, a cupboard of oat cakes and figs, cups with blue and white stripe. When he died and the studio was dismantled, I took the Morris curtains and tea set. There was a perfectly neat, perfectly small bathroom, bath and sink. Next to it, the same size, a bedroom with single bed where after lunch he'd take forty winks. His desk was fitted in a corner, his typewriter and swivel chair, a drawing of his Uncle Ivar, handsome in the library at Inveraray with pipe in his mouth, now sits on my desk with the calendar in its silver frame. There were tiny brass animals on the windowsill, there were pine steps up into the gallery that felt like a tall ship's galley, its pitched walls cleverly lined with paintings of women in rustling dresses, velvet ribbons at their throats, faces like mine. There, our Christmas presents were stored, and I passed them along into his arms and we took them, pile by stacked precarious pile down the outside stairs to the waiting Subaru. The cosy studio, the sudden rush and chill of winter stairs, my boots leaving mud, and when we were finished, we stood at the top, the half-glazed door locked by him. The banister had a ridge and valley to the wall, it made for a slide for a small and well-placed set of keys, teeth up, stretched out, keyring in the middle. At the bottom by the final door was a green Hunter wellington, an old one of his, exactly placed if you were lucky or skilled, and let's see, as he smiles and says, *Off you go then,* and I let go. Away the bunch of keys, sliding inexorably faster, twenty steps or more, flying downward, will they do it, and the micro perfect second's silence as we watch and they leap from end into air, choose success or failure, disappear with damp black thud into the boot, our cheers already echoing the thin false walls, the windows frosted. He was a man of little games punctuating moments of a life lived carefully, this moment now as we drive like royalty along narrow lanes, hedgerows bare, bracken bent and brown, our Christmas presents piled in the back, the low-beamed cottage coming into view, waiting hands.

CRACKERS

I am surrounded by cats, I always have been, I am half cat. In London, Tabitha Twitchit kept me going, in Sussex, Jerry and Sirie. Rosalee Parks sits beside me as I write. Kenny slept with her paws on my shoulder, in the early hours of this morning I woke to her purring. Did you know these Recovery Diaries are coming to end? I do, tomorrow is their last day, and this, the penultimate, feels blank. Each time as I've gone to bed, I've not known what I'll write when I face the page the next morning, I've always said, turn up and it will come, but today, nothing. Where were we? Riding like royalty in the Subaru to waiting hands, my mother in the kitchen wrestling turkey, the annual row over whether to open presents before or after lunch; it was always after. Yesterday as I meditated, I saw my parts and allies crowding their faces at the window to watch me in the sitting room, we each had a chair, my gifts were piled at the settle, I remember the year I got my marble run and built it in the upstairs corridor, the stretch of coloured plastic shoots and twirls on brown carpet, from bedroom door to stairs, a city of connection, in the way of everyone; oblivious to their stepping over, stepping round, I was left alone to play. And I remembered how the beam at the end on the left was so low even I as a child had to bend my head to get to bathroom or loo, how I always saw the head of a blond man in the lavatory when I lifted the lid, how I'd flush, and duck, and run, making it to the stairs before the flush was over. The way into these memories is often incongruous and silly, always the risk that I'll be thought crackers, it can be easy to miss or dismiss, *I can't possibly write about that*, but I've learnt that with every image offered, there's a crumb line leading somewhere. A blond head of a man in a loo. A fear always there. So, my parts and allies crowd their faces at the window as I open my presents while in the dining room the table is set for Christmas lunch, a table bomb from Harrods, crackers arranged at each plate, we will cross our arms and pull, we will put on paper hats and tell jokes. My sister will refuse Brussel sprouts and be made to eat *just one.* My mother will come in with a pudding on fire, the blue flames lighting up the porcelain dish, her fingers, the exhaustion I never recognised, not knowing what it is to do Christmas for a family of many and granny who drove my father mad, always asking him the same question, *What are you writing now?,* and he'd ignore her. And the Christmas holidays were coming to an end, the return to London looming, the severed head of the blonde man because in this time-warp recovery, one thing can be understood: that what I was seeing was the work of my parts and allies who I only came to recognise now, but now being then, their work was done. Rosie in her jeans and fierceness took a sword to his memory, a decapitation of his power, I didn't know as I lifted the lid and peed and ran, we can change our past experience. Not the events, but the emotional aftermath. I will stay with my marble run, they will stay with their faces crowding the window, the colours and the twirling glass balls that I set off when I sit down to type. Recovery takes forever.

THE SHELF LIFE OF GRIEF

A friend, a seismic tragedy, hearts irreparably broken, and a few years had passed when a family member said, *Must you bring that up again?* This story told to me, and it made me think about the shelf life of grief, whether the world says there is one, and how there isn't for the person grieving. Everything must end except feelings which don't, which go on like recovery forever. These diaries have changed me. I didn't know how they'd play out. There's been a freedom here to move around, from fairy story to aging, sobriety to a tall, cold house in London falling down and Christmas in a low-beamed cottage that I didn't want to leave, there's been memories and rooms described and a cast list of parts reclaimed, and new friends made and I don't know what comes next except the need to make space for it. The work goes on; more than any other note I've had over these 108 posts, it's been that they've felt real, and that being the highest praise, I'm going to take it. My friend of the seismic tragedy must live with their feelings every day, and so must I and so must you, there is no shelf life, only distance from events that hurt you. I said to some youth recently, *You can freewheel until fifty, and then you've got to start pedalling,* because once you're over that hump all the stuff un-dealt with rises up. I'm amazed at how much I was carrying around unhidden to everyone but me who was oblivious except for all the dysfunction, the broken relationships, the inability to stay in the room. These diaries are a record of the work, and I've learnt to stay with uncomfortable feelings, and writing every morning, I've learnt to stay in the room. The cat is asleep on the table, there are coats and jumpers thrown on the sofa, friends are staying; last night a dinner out, back late, the joy of parts of my life meeting, how I am me irrespective of company, the roles that I've played in the past that are dead I don't grieve for. There's a lot to be said for getting old. My shoulder hurts and this week I'll see my friend with the magic hands and the work, inexorably, continues. I am digging my way out. But everything like art must end and this is it, an end to these diaries. It's been fun. You know when there's a big goodbye, and you hug everyone and kiss some people twice by mistake and go back for another last-minute conversation with someone else and finally rush out the door waving and halfway down the path you realise you've forgotten your keys?

ACKNOWLEDGEMENTS

Thank you, all you people who found me on Substack, read my words as they appeared each day, sent supportive, wonderful comments my way, let me know again and again that my words mattered, and I wasn't alone. It was because of you that this work gained momentum, took form, found its feet and grew. You know who you are. Give yourselves a hug.

Thanks also to my friends and family, always there for me, and especially to Andy, who put up with me slipping not so quietly out of bed at four each morning to write. Who'd love a writer? You would, you do, and I am ever grateful.

This book is printed on paper from sustainable sources managed under the Forest Stewardship Council (FSC) scheme.

It has been printed in the UK to reduce transportation miles and their impact upon the environment.

For every new title that Troubador publishes, we plant a tree to offset CO_2, partnering with the More Trees scheme.

For more about how Troubador offsets its environmental impact, see www.troubador.co.uk/sustainability-and-community